BUDGET JUSTIFICATIONS

The United States
Department of the Interior

and Performance Information
Fiscal Year 2014

NATURAL RESOURCE DAMAGE ASSESSMENT AND RESTORATION PROGRAM

References to the *2013 Full Yr. CR* signify annualized amounts appropriated in P.L. 112-175, the Continuing Appropriations Act. These amounts are the 2012 enacted numbers annualized through the end of FY 2013 with a 0.612 percent across-the-board increase for discretionary programs. Exceptions to this include Wildland Fire Management, which received an anomaly in the 2013 CR to fund annual operations at $726.5 million. The *2013 Full Yr. CR* does not incorporate reductions associated with the Presidential sequestration order issued in accordance with section 251A of the Balanced Budget and Emergency Deficit Control Act, as amended (BBEDCA), 2 U.S.C. 109a. This column is provided for reference only.

DEPARTMENT OF THE INTERIOR

Restoration Program
Assessment & Restoration Program

Fiscal Year 2014 Budget Justifications

TABLE OF CONTENTS

Appropriation: Natural Resource Damage Assessment and Restoration

NATURAL RESOURCE DAMAGE ASSESSMENT AND RESTORATION PROGRAM

GENERAL STATEMENT

FY 2014 Budget Request:

The Restoration Program's Fiscal Year 2014 request for current appropriations is $12,539,000, an increase of $6,286,000 over the 2012 enacted level of $6,253,000. The request supports significant increases in on-the-ground restoration, and allocations of the growing balance of funds recovered in settlements to implement approved restoration plans. This will be accomplished consistent with a detailed programmatic analysis and development of a strategic plan currently underway, aimed at restructuring Restoration Program activities to maximize restoration outcomes. This analysis will seek to identify staffing constraints and process bottlenecks in the course of achieving restoration in coordination with our co-trustee partners. Using the requested increase, staff will be added to the Program's Restoration Support Unit and allocated to bureaus and offices to accelerate restoration activities in accord with this expanding workload.

Over the last three years, the DOI Restoration Fund has received an average of over $150 million each year in restoration settlements and cooperative damage assessment funds. A large majority of these recoveries are shared jointly with other Federal, State, and tribal co-trustees, and as such, the Department cannot use them unilaterally. A number of long-running damage assessments cases have recently settled and others are in settlement negotiations. This recent heightened influx of settlement funds is expected to continue as additional cases settle , and thus requires that the Restoration Program (along with involved DOI bureaus) examine its program infrastructure and staffing on a Department-wide basis, to best position the Program to deal with a growing pool of restoration funds. The need for Program restructuring and additional staff resources will be further exacerbated by anticipated additional funds for ecological restoration from Restore Act activities and from a settlement for natural resource injury in the Deepwater Horizon oil spill.

The potential benefits associated with this budget request are significant, for both injured natural resources and the American public. With nearly a half billion dollars in settlement funds currently residing in the DOI Restoration Fund, and more settlements on the horizon, moving forward deliberately and strategically in the implementation of restoration actions at dozens of sites nationwide will produce benefits, both ecologically and economically.

Total 2014 Budget Request
(Dollars in Thousands)

Budget Authority	2012 Actual	2013 Full Year CR	2014 Budget Request
Current	6,253	6,291	12,539
Mandatory	125,367	90,000	80,000
TOTAL	**131,620**	**96,291**	**92,539**
FTE	*9*	*12*	*20*

Fiscal Year 2013 and 2014 fixed costs of $230,000 are fully funded at the request level.

In addition, the request includes an estimate of $80.0 million in permanent funds for DOI bureaus and its Federal, State, and tribal co-trustees, which result from negotiated legal settlement agreements and cooperative damage assessments with responsible parties.

Executive Summary

The mission of the Natural Resource Damage Assessment and Restoration Program (Restoration Program) is to restore natural resources injured as a result of oil spills or hazardous substance releases into the environment. In partnership with other affected Federal, State, and tribal trustee agencies, damage assessments provide the basis for determining the restoration needs that address the public's loss and use of these resources. Cooperation with its co-trustees and partners, and where possible, with the responsible parties, is an important component of meeting the Restoration Program's core mission.

As authorized by the Comprehensive Environmental Response, Compensation and Liability Act (CERCLA or Superfund), the Clean Water Act (CWA), and the Oil Pollution Act of 1990 (OPA), injuries to natural resources that the Department of the Interior manages or controls are assessed, and appropriate restoration projects are identified in contemplation of negotiated settlements or in rare cases, litigation with potentially responsible parties. Recoveries, in cash or in-kind services, from the potentially responsible parties are then used to finance or implement the restoration of the injured resources, pursuant to a publicly reviewed restoration plan.

The Office of Restoration and Damage Assessment (Program Office) manages the confluence of the technical, ecological, biological, legal, and economic disciplines and coordinates the efforts of six bureaus and three offices to accomplish this mission. The Program has a nationwide presence encompassing nearly the full span of natural and cultural resources for which the

Secretary of the Interior has trust responsibility. Each bureau has its unique natural resource trusteeship and brings its expertise to bear on relevant sites. The Restoration Program is a truly integrated Departmental program, drawing upon the interdisciplinary strengths of its various bureaus and offices, while eliminating or minimizing redundant bureau-level bureaucratic and administrative operations.

The **Bureau of Indian Affairs** is responsible for the administration and management over 55 million surface acres and 57 million acres of sub-surface minerals estates held in trust by the United States for American Indians, Indian Tribes, and Alaska Natives, and provides assistance to 566 federally-recognized tribal governments to help protect water, natural resources and land rights.

The **Bureau of Land Management** administers 248 million acres of Federal land and 700 million acres of subsurface mineral estate, located primarily in 12 western states, including Alaska, characterized by grasslands, forests, deserts, coastline, and arctic tundra. The BLM sustains the ecological and economic health, diversity, and productivity of these public lands for the use and enjoyment of present and future generations.

Working in 17 states west of the Mississippi River, the **Bureau of Reclamation** manages 476 dams and 348 reservoirs covering more than 6.6 million acres associated with irrigation projects to protect local economies and preserve natural resources and ecosystems through the management and effective use of water resources.

The **U.S. Fish & Wildlife Service** conserves, protects and enhances fish, wildlife, and plants and their habitats and manages over 150 million acres within 561 National Wildlife Refuges, other refuge units, and 38 wetland management districts for the continuing benefit of the American people, providing primary trusteeship for migratory birds and over 2,054 threatened and endangered species.

The **National Park Service** preserves unimpaired the natural and cultural resources and values of the 84 million acres of land and 4.5 million acres of oceans, lakes, and reservoirs of the 398 units of the national park system, and conserves the scenery and the natural and historic objects and the wildlife of these special places for the enjoyment, education, and inspiration of current and future generations.

In addition to the five bureaus with primary trust resource management activities, the U.S. Geological Survey (USGS), the Office of the Secretary, and the Office of the Solicitor play key roles in making the Restoration Program a fully integrated Departmental program. The Office of the Solicitor provides legal advice, USGS provides technical scientific support, and the Office of Policy Analysis provides economic analytical expertise to the Program at both a national policy and individual case management levels. The Office of Environmental Policy and Compliance provides a link to response and remedial activities associated with oil spills or chemical releases.

The Department, through its bureaus, conducts every damage assessment and restoration case in partnership with co-trustees at various levels (Federal, State, and tribal), and all restoration plans must undergo public review and be approved by affected State and tribal governments. The Restoration Program serves as a model of collaboration in its day-to-day operations and partnerships that have been developed with tribal, State, and other Federal co-trustees, as well as with non-governmental conservation organizations and industry.

Overview

The FY 2014 budget request for the Natural Resource Damage Assessment and Restoration Program totals $12,539,000, an increase of $6,286,000 over the 2012 enacted level. The requested increase supports the following program initiatives:

1. Restoration Support (+$4.2 million), is focused at providing additional staff and program capacity to significantly increase the amount of restoration implementation across the country, and to ensure the effective utilization of the growing balance of restoration settlement funds in the DOI Restoration Fund. An increase in the number of dedicated program staff focused exclusively on implementing restoration will result in marked increases in the amount of acres and stream /shoreline miles being restored, along with attendant ecological and economic benefits for the American public.

2. Onshore Oil Spill Preparedness (+$2.2 million), will allow the Department to develop the tools and contingency plans necessary to deal with inland oil spills. Conventional energy resources will continue to remain an important component as the Department moves forward in implementing the New Energy Frontier Initiative. Domestic oil and gas production and transportation are likely to continue at high, and potentially increasing, levels. New forms of transportation entering into the industry (e.g., tank cars on high-speed rail and pipelines carrying tar sands/bitumen oil) pose new risks and challenges to spill planners and responders.

Secretarial Initiatives

America's Great Outdoors (AGO)

On April 16, 2010, President Obama announced the *America's Great Outdoors* (AGO) initiative, launching the development of a 21st century conservation and recreation agenda. The result is a call for a grassroots approach to protecting our lands and waters and connecting all Americans to their natural and cultural heritage. The AGO initiative seeks to empower all Americans to share in the responsibility to conserve, restore, and provide better access to our lands and waters in order to leave a healthy, vibrant outdoor legacy for generations to come. Funding for the initiative is broadly defined to capture programs that are key to attaining conservation goals. That includes funding to operate and maintain our public lands; expand and improve recreational opportunities at the state and local level; protect cultural resources; and conserve and restore land, water, and native species.

The Restoration Program has no discretionary appropriated funds that specifically tie to the *America's Great Outdoors* initiative. However, many of the projects, funded with permanent funds, accomplish resource objectives that are consistent with the spirit and intent of the AGO initiative. A large percentage of DOI and its Federal, State, and tribal co-trustee partners' restoration actions and accomplishments using settlement funds recovered through the Restoration Program are targeted toward the restoration, acquisition, or protection of public lands, creation of recreational opportunities, and the restoration of landscapes and trust species.

Administration's Management Agenda

Campaign to Cut Waste Over the last three years, the Administration has implemented a series of management reforms to curb uncontrolled growth in contract spending, terminate poorly performing information technology projects, deploy state of the art fraud detection tools, focus agency leaders on achieving ambitious improvements in high priority areas, and open Government up to the public to increase accountability and accelerate innovation.

In November 2011, President Obama issued an Executive Order reinforcing these performance and management reforms and the achievement of efficiencies and cost-cutting across the government. This Executive Order identifies specific savings as part of the Administration's Campaign to Cut Waste to achieve a 20 percent reduction in administrative spending from 2010 to 2013, and then sustain these savings in 2014. Each agency is directed to establish a plan to reduce the combined costs associated with travel, employee information technology devices, printing, executive fleet services, and extraneous promotional items and other areas.

The Department of the Interior's goal is on target to reduce administrative spending by $217 million from 2010 levels by the end of 2013, and to sustain these savings in 2014. To meet this goal, the Department is leading efforts to reduce waste and create efficiencies by reviewing projected and actual administrative spending to allocate efficiency targets for bureaus and Departmental offices to achieve the 20 percent target. Additional details on the Campaign to Cut Waste can be found at: http://www.whitehouse.gov/the-press-office/2011/11/09/executive-order-promoting-efficient-spending.

Through the end of 2012, the Restoration Program and its components across the Department had met its Campaign to Cut Waste target goals. The continued and increased use of SharePoint collaboration tools will continue to allow the program to minimize its travel costs in 2013 and 2014.

DOI Strategic Plan:

The FY 2011-2016 DOI Strategic Plan, in compliance with the principles of the GPRA Modernization Act of 2010, provides a collection of mission objectives, goals, strategies and corresponding metrics that provide an integrated and focused approach for tracking performance across a wide range of DOI programs. While the DOI Strategic Plan for FY 2011 – FY 2016 is the foundational structure for the description of program performance measurement and planning for the FY 2014 President's Budget, further details for achieving the Strategic Plan's goals are presented in the DOI Annual Performance Plan and Report (APP&R). Bureau and program specific plans for FY 2014 are fully consistent with the goals, outcomes, and measures described in the FY 2011-2016 version of the DOI Strategic Plan and related implementation information in the Annual Performance Plan and Report (APP&R).

Total 2014 Budget Request
(Dollars in Thousands)

Budget Authority	2012 Actual	2013 Full Year CR	2014 Budget Request
Discretionary	6,253	6,291	12,539
Mandatory	125,367	90,000	80,000
TOTAL	131,620	96,291	92,539
FTE	9	12	20

Program Performance Summary

All activities within the Restoration Program (damage assessment, restoration support, oil spill preparedness, and program management) support resource restoration either directly or as necessary steps on the road to restoration of injured natural resources under the trusteeship of the Department of the Interior. These restoration activities contribute towards Mission Area 1 / Goal No.1 in the Department's Strategic Plan, namely to <u>Provide Natural and Cultural Resource Protection and Experiences/Protect America's Landscapes</u>. As is also the case with the Department's *America's Great Outdoors* initiative, the Program's restoration of injured natural resources includes activities as varied as partnerships to acquire high-value habitats; improved stewardship of Federal, State and tribal lands; and landscape-level conservation in key ecosystems.

In addition, the Program's damage assessment and restoration activities undertaken with tribal co-trustees support the *Strengthening Tribal Nations* initiative by working government to government as equal partners to restore tribal natural resources. The Program also seeks opportunities wherever possible to involve young people, either in hands-on restoration activities or outdoor classroom experiences, in support of the Youth in the Great Outdoors Initiative. For example, fostering a connection between people and restored habitats is a goal of the Sudbury River Schools program, funded with $90,000 from the Nyanza settlement. Members of the Massachusetts Audubon Society will work with at least two schools in five Sudbury River communities over the course of three years to educate students and teachers about native plants and wildlife through various studies and visits to the river.

As required by the Government Performance and Results Act of 1993, the Department recently published its Strategic Plan for Fiscal Years 2011 – 2016. This current Strategic Plan updated the prior plan (FY2007 – 2012) and includes a simpler and more strategic set of goals and more finite and focused performance measures. NRDAR Program performance is measured and reported respectively by the bureau that is the lead agency in any given case, described in each bureau's budget justification, and consolidated with performance measures from other programs in reporting the strategic outcomes. This budget request also continues to report a summary of on-the-ground performance, focusing on acres and miles of habitat restored. Performance measures reported here are not added to the Departmental strategic reporting in order to avoid potential issues of double-counting.

2014 Program Performance

In 2014, the Program expects to see measurable increases in the amount of restoration being achieved, notably through the Program's performance indicators of acres restored and stream / shoreline miles restored. A lesser, secondary measure tracking the movement of settlement funds transferred out of the Restoration Fund to DOI bureaus and involved co-trustees will also be monitored. These increases will result from the additional Restoration Support staff and resources contained in the 2014 budget request. The addition of new dedicated staff focused on supporting on-the-ground restoration will pay benefits within the first year.

The Program will continue to review, develop and implement guidance and regulatory reforms that directly address process improvements recommended over the past several years by field practitioners, co-trustees, and key stakeholders. The program will also continue to work closely with Federal, State, and tribal co-trustees and other interested parties to gather the most up to date information needed for guidance development. These improvements address four major policy areas: injury quantification, damage determination, analysis of restoration alternatives, and restoration implementation. Once implemented, the recommendations will lead to improved processes and tools to achieve long-term restoration goals that support the Department's mission and overall goal to protect the Nation's natural, cultural, and recreational resources.

In 2014, the Program will continue to focus its activities in support of trust resource restoration, and will, through the addition of additional Restoration Support staffing and resources, and the implementation of a program strategic plan, see increased restoration outputs and outcomes. Fiscal Year 2014 planned performance targets include the restoration of 22,500 acres and 180 stream or shoreline miles, increases of 3,750 acres (+20%) and 15 stream / shoreline miles (+9%), respectively over FY 2013 strategic plan goals. Attainment of these goals will be accomplished by the Department and its co-trustees through the use of funds or in-kind services received in settlement of damage claims with responsible parties.

The Program also monitors the amount of funds disbursed from the Restoration Fund to the bureaus and co-trustees to implement on-the-ground restoration projects. In Fiscal Year 2012, the Restoration Program released $63.3 million to trustee agencies for restoration activities, surpassing the annual amounts released in each of the previous four years (2008 – 2011). To date, through the first half of Fiscal Year 2013 the program has released over $38 million for restoration.

Restoration program performance measures and accomplishments in all four program activities (Damage Assessment, Restoration Support, Onshore Oil Spill Preparedness, and Program Management) are singularly focused on one goal, the increased restoration of acres and stream / shoreline miles. Such restoration creates or protects habitat for injured biological communities to recuperate, thrive and flourish. Programmatic performance accomplishments at the activity level are but a step leading to the implementation of restoration actions. Within the Damage Assessment activity, data is collected annually on all Departmentally-funded cases, which enables the Program to monitor the progress of cases through the assessment process to settlement, using measures such as number of cases reaching various milestones, numbers of cooperative assessments with industry, and number of cases settled. In 2014, the Program will continue to work with the USGS on a restoration science initiative to develop protocols and metrics to better measure the ecological outcomes of restoration activities, including measures relating to carbon capture and climate change.

The Restoration Program's performance goals reflect continued progress funded with monies and in-kind actions recovered in settlement from responsible parties, and not appropriated funds. Appropriated discretionary funds are used to fund damage assessments, administer the program, conduct onshore oil spill preparedness, and provide technical support. Recent successful settlements of natural resource damage claims have increased the balance of and drawn attention to the NRDAR Fund, especially under the current economic funding restraints. Settlements in fiscal years 2010 and 2011, including the largest NRDAR settlement from a bankruptcy claim (ASARCO, $180 million) and several other multi-million dollar settlements added $333 million to the fund, equal to the settlement receipts of the first 15 years of the Program from 1992 through 2006. As of the end of December 2012, there was $455 million in settlement funds in the DOI Restoration Fund that are dedicated for restoration activities that will allow the program to continue moving forward towards its long term restoration goals.

Restoration accomplishments in acres and stream/shoreline miles restored often fluctuate from year-to-year, the result of a complex process in which numerous trustee councils across the Nation are moving forward in identifying specific opportunities for restoration consistent with approved restoration plans, but which generally cannot be scheduled or readily anticipated on a site-specific basis. The year-to-year variability in performance shown on the following table reflects the pace of restoration which is greatly influenced by factors outside the Department's control, such as finding cooperative landowners or willing sellers.

The bureaus will continue to collect, validate, and verify the performance data before reporting to the Program. In addition, the Program Office will continue to track internally the progress of cases from start to finish using measures such as increased numbers of restoration plans drafted, finalized, and in stages of implementation; increased numbers of restorations completed; increased numbers of cooperative assessments with industry; and increased funding leveraged from restoration partnerships.

The increasingly common use of cooperative assessments is expected to continue, thus minimizing the chance of adversarial confrontations with responsible parties, and thus allowing case teams to move more quickly to settlement and restoration. In addition, the Office is working with the bureaus to continue to enhance internal and external restoration partnerships and to make greater use of existing watershed, landscape, or flyway scale restoration plans to jumpstart NRD restoration implantation where appropriate. In the longer term, regulatory, policy and operational improvements arising from practitioner, co-trustee, and stakeholder recommendations will lead to better, more efficient damage assessments, which will lead to quicker and more effective restorations, positioning the Restoration Program to achieve its long-term strategic plan goals.

FY 2013 Program Evaluation - There are a number of efforts currently underway that will help the Restoration Program meet its performance goals for 2014. During 2013, working with its Executive Board, the Program will complete an independent program evaluation, focusing on how the Program can best align its resources and activities to achieve additional support to accelerate the completion of restoration projects. The results of the program evaluation will be used to focus the funding requested in 2014 on areas that will increase accomplishments within the Restoration Support activity.

Goal Performance Table

Appropriation: Natural Resource Damage Assessment and Restoration

Mission Area 1: Provide natural and cultural resource protection and experiences

Goal #1: Protect America's landscapes

Supporting Performance Measures	Type	2009 Actual	2010 Actual	2011 Actual	2012 Plan	2012 Actual	2013 Plan	2014 Request	Change from 2013 Plan to 2014	Long-Term Target 2016
Strategy #1: Improve land and water health by restoring wetlands and uplands that support trust natural resources that have been injured by oil spills or releases of hazardous substances										
Number of acres restored or enhanced to achieve desired habitat conditions to support trust species conservation	A	41,183	68,834	87,709	15,000	97,813	18,750	22,500	20%	30,000
Comments: Year to year variability is expected based on variability of timing and settlement amounts.										
Contributing Programs: NRDAR, FWS Environmental Contaminants, NPS, BIA, BLM, BOR, USGS, SOL, OS/Policy Analysis, other Federal, State, and tribal co-trustees										
Strategy #2: Improve land and water health by restoring riparian, stream, ans shoreline areas that support trust natural resources that have been injured by oil spills or releases of hazardous substances										
Number of stream or shoreline miles restored or enhanced to achieve desired habitat conditions to support trust species conservation	A	186	377	401	150	409	165	180	9%	210
Comments: Year to year variability is expected based on variability of timing and settlement amounts.										
Contributing Programs: NRDAR, FWS Environmental Contaminants, NPS, BIA, BLM, BOR, USGS, SOL, OS/Policy Analysis, other Federal, State, and tribal co-trustees										

Note: The actual and planned acres and miles presented in this table are included among the performance results and targets presented in the Performance Budgets of the bureaus. As such, in order to avoid double-counting, these acres and miles are not included in the Department's aggregate results calculations or performance projections.

The DOI Office of Restoration and Damage Assessment (ORDA) manages the Restoration Program, and currently consists of twelve (12) direct FTE. They are the Office Director and eleven staff: including the Deputy Office Director for Restoration, the Assistant Office Director for Operations, the Budget Officer/Restoration Fund Manager, and a budget analyst located in its Washington, DC headquarters; four staff Restoration Support specialists located in Denver, Colorado; and operations staffers in San Francisco, California and Philadelphia, Pennsylvania. The following organization chart goes beyond the small number of people in the Program Management Office and reflects the integrated management structure of the Program as a whole, with the interrelated components of six bureaus, the Office of the Solicitor, and two offices within the Office of the Secretary.

Restoration Program
Natural Resource Damage Assessment & Restoration Program

Assistant Secretary - Policy, Management, and Budget

Deputy Assistant Secretary – Policy and International Affairs

ORDA Office Director --- **Executive Board**

Asst. Office Director **Restoration Fund Manager** **Deputy Office Director**

Operations Staff

Restoration Support Unit

Technical Support
Economics
Office of Policy Analysis
Science
U.S. Geological Survey
Law
Office of the Solicitor

Workgroup

Fish and Wildlife Service
National Park Service
Bureau of Indian Affairs
Bureau of Land Management
Bureau of Reclamation

The Restoration Program reports to the Deputy Assistant Secretary – Policy and International Affairs, under the Assistant Secretary - Policy, Management, and Budget (AS-PMB). There is also a "Restoration Executive Board" representative at the assistant director level for BIA, BLM, BOR, FWS and NPS; a Deputy Associate Solicitor, and the Director of the Office of Environmental Policy and Compliance. The Restoration Executive Board is responsible for overseeing policy direction and approving allocation of resources.

Summary of Requirements Table
(Dollars in Thousands)

Appropriation: Natural Resource Damage Assessment and Restoration

Comparison by Activity / Subactivity

Activity	2013 CR Level (Annualized) FTE	Amount	2012 Enacted FTE	Amount	Fixed Costs (+/-) FTE	Amount	Internal Transfer FTE	Amount	Program Changes (+/-) FTE	Amount	2014 Budget Request FTE	Amount	Inc. (+)/ Dec(-) from 2012 Enacted FTE	Amount
APPROPRIATED FUNDS														
Damage Assessments	0	3,177	0	3,737	0	+24	0	-570	0	+0	0	3,191	0	-546
Restoration Support	4	1,160	2	613	0	+9		+570	+9	+3,605	11	4,797	+9	+4,184
Oil Spill Preparedness	0	0	0	0	0	0			+2	+2,200	2	2,200	+2	+2,200
Program Management	8	1,954	7	1,903	0	+197			0	+251	7	2,351	0	+448
Total, Appropriation	**12**	**6,291**	**9**	**6,253**	**0**	**+230**		**0**	**+11**	**+6,056**	**20**	**12,539**	**+11**	**+6,286**
PERMANENT FUNDS (RECEIPTS)														
Damage Assessments		20,000		27,472		0				-13,572		13,900		-13,572
Restoration														
[Prince William Sound Restoration]		5,500		8,474						-2,474		6,000		-2,474
[Other Restoration]		64,400		89,482						-29,482		60,000		-29,482
Program Management		100		65						+35		100		+35
Subtotal, Gross Receipts	**0**	**90,000**	**0**	**125,493**	**0**	**0**		**0**	**0**	**-45,493**	**0**	**80,000**	**0**	**-45,493**
Transfers Out		**-8,050**		**-7,279**		**0**				**0**		**-8,050**		**-771**
Total, Net Receipts		**81,950**		**118,214**		**0**				**-45,493**		**71,950**		**-46,264**

13

Natural Resource Damage Assessment and Restoration Program

Justification of Fixed Costs and Internal Realignments
(Dollars In Thousands)

Other Fixed Cost Changes and Projections	PY (2012) to BY (2014) Change
Change in Number of Paid Days	+16
The combined fixed cost estimate includes an adjustment for one additional paid day between FY2012 and FY2013. The number of paid days do not change between FY2013 and FY2014.	
Pay Raise	+44
The PY column reflects the total pay raise changes as reflected in the the PY President's Budget. The BY Change column reflects the total pay raise changes between FY2012-FY2014.	
Employer Share of Federal Health Benefit Plans	+18
The change reflects expected increases in employer's share of Federal Health Benefit Plans.	
Departmental Working Capital Fund	+24
The change reflects expected changes in the charges for centrally billed Department services and other services through the Working Capital Fund. These charges are displayed in the Budget Justification for Department Management.	
Rental Payments	+128
The adjustment is for changes in the costs payable to General Services Administration (GSA) and others resulting from changes in rates for office and non-office space as estimated by GSA, as well as the rental costs of other currently occupied space. These costs include building security; in the case of GSA space, these are paid to Department of Homeland Security (DHS). Costs of mandatory office relocations, i.e. relocations in cases where due to external events there is no alternative but to vacate the currently occupied space, are also included.	

Internal Realignments and Non-Policy/Program Changes (Net-Zero)	BY (2014) (+/-)
Restoration Support	
The Restoration Program includes in its 2013 Operating Plan an internal transfer of funds between the Damage Assessments activity and the Restoration Support activity. This internal adjustment directs additional effort towards increasing the volume of on-going restoration implementation.	
Damage Assessments	-570
Restoration Support	+570

Natural Resource Damage Assessment and Restoration Program

Appropriations Language

NATURAL RESOURCE DAMAGE ASSESSMENT FUND

To conduct natural resource damage assessment, restoration activities, and onshore oil spill preparedness by the Department of the Interior necessary to carry out the provisions of the Comprehensive Environmental Response, Compensation, and Liability Act, as amended (42 U.S.C. 9601 et seq.), the Federal Water Pollution Control Act, as amended (33 U.S.C. 1251 et seq.), the Oil Pollution Act of 1990 (33 U.S.C. 2701 et seq.), and Public Law 101-337, as amended (16 U.S.C. 19jj et seq.), $12,539,000, to remain available until expended.

Note - - A full-year 2013 appropriation for this account was not enacted at the time the budget was prepared; therefore, the budget assumes the account is operating under the Continuing Appropriations Resolution, 2013 (P.L. 112-175). The amounts included for 2013 reflect the annualized level provided by the continuing resolution.

Justification of Proposed Language Change

1. Addition: "…and onshore oil spill preparedness"

This new language is needed to authorize a new activity proposed within the NRDAR program to improve Department-wide spill response preparedness, including review of spill contingency plans and participation in response drills and exercises.

Authorizing Statutes:

Comprehensive Environmental Response, Compensation, and Liability Act*, as amended, *(42 U.S.C 9601 et seq.). Section 106 of the Act authorizes the President to clean up hazardous substance sites directly, or obtain cleanup by a responsible party through enforcement actions. Trustees for natural resources may assess and recover damages for injury to natural resources from releases of hazardous substances and use the damages for restoration, replacement or acquisition of equivalent natural resources. Provides permanent authorization to appropriate receipts from responsible parties.

Federal Water Pollution Control Act (Clean Water Act)*, as amended, *(33 U.S.C. 1251-1387). Authorizes trustees for natural resources to assess and recover damages for injuries to natural resources resulting from the discharge of oil into or upon the navigable waters of the United States, adjoining shorelines, the waters of the contiguous zone, or in connection with activities under the *Outer Continental Shelf Lands Act* or the *Deepwater Port Act of 1974*, or which may affect natural resources belonging to, appertaining to, or under the exclusive management authority of the United States.

Oil Pollution Act of 1990, (33 U.S.C. 2701 et seq.) Amends the *Federal Water Pollution Control Act*, and authorizes trustee(s) of natural resources to present a claim for and to recover damages for injuries to natural resources from each responsible party for a vessel or facility from which oil is discharged, or which poses a substantial threat of discharge of oil, into or upon the navigable waters or adjoining shorelines or the exclusive zone.

Public Law 101-337, (16 U.S.C. 19jj). Provides that response costs and damages recovered under it or amounts recovered under any statute as a result of damage to any Federal resource within a unit of the National Park System shall be retained and used for response costs, damage assessments, restoration, and replacements. Liability for damages under this Act is in addition to any other liability that may arise under other statutes.

Interior and Related Agencies Appropriation Act, 1992 (P.L. 102-154). Provides permanent authorization for receipts for damage assessment and restoration activities to be available without further appropriation until expended.

Dire Emergency Supplemental Appropriations for Fiscal Year 1992 (P.L. 102-229). Provides that the Fund's receipts are authorized to be invested and available until expended. Also provides that amounts received by United States in settlement of *U.S. v Exxon Corp. et al.* in FY 1992 and thereafter be deposited into the Fund.

Interior and Related Agencies Appropriation Act, 1998 (P.L. 104-134). Provides authority to make transfers of settlement funds to other federal trustees and payments to non-federal trustees.

ACTIVITY: DAMAGE ASSESSMENT

Example of migratory bird killed at copper mine tailings pond (FWS Photo)

Appropriation: Natural Resource Damage Assessment		*2013 Full Yr. CR (PL. 112-175)*	2012 Enacted	Fixed Costs	Internal Transfers (+/-)	Program Changes (+/-)	2014 Request
Activity: Damage Assessment	$000	*3,177*	3,737	+24	-570	0	3,191
	FTE	*0*	0	0	0	0	0

Note: FY2012 FTE reflects actual usage.   All FTE use is reported by bureaus.

Explanation of 2014 Internal Transfer:

Damage Assessment (-$570,000 / 0 FTE) - In the 2013 Continuing Resolution (P.L. 112-175) Operating Plan, the Restoration Program made an internal budget transfer, moving $570,000 from the Damage Assessment activity to the Restoration Support activity. This transfer was made to provide additional resources for supporting the case teams and trustee councils across the Nation in the planning and implementation of restoration actions in settled cases. The decrease to the Damage Assessment activity will be offset with recovered assessment costs from settled cases. Recent settlements of previously-funded damage assessment cases has resulted in the recovery of past assessment costs that will be used to fund cases going forward, in lieu of appropriated funds so that the total available for damage assessment activities remains level.

Activity Overview:

Damage assessment activities are the critical first step taken by the Department on the long journey to achieving restoration of natural resources injured through the release of oil or hazardous substances. The source and magnitude of injury must first be identified, investigated, and thoroughly understood if the subsequent restoration is to be effective. Through the damage assessment process, physical and scientific evidence of natural resource injury is documented, which then forms the basis for the Department's claim for appropriate compensation (or in-kind services) to compensate the American public for the loss and use of those injured resources. The resulting restoration settlements allow the Restoration Program to then restore those injured trust resources, in concert with other affected natural resource trustees. Damage assessment activities support the Department's performance outcome goals of protecting the Nation's natural and cultural resources. Information regarding the nature, pathway, and magnitude of the injury, and the means by which they are determined, also help establish the focus of the subsequent restoration plans and influence the determination of when those goals have been successfully reached.

Damage assessment cases are conducted by one or more of the five resource management bureaus within the Department: (Fish and Wildlife Service; National Park Service; Bureau of Land Management; Bureau of Indian Affairs; and Bureau of Reclamation). All FTE involved in supporting this activity are allocation FTE, located in the Departmental bureaus, there are no direct FTE within the Program Office. Economic analytical support is provided by the Office of Policy Analysis, scientific / technical analysis and support from the U.S. Geological Survey, and legal counsel from the Office of the Solicitor. In nearly all cases, assessment activities are carried out in partnership with other affected Federal, State, and/or tribal co-trustees. These partnerships have proven advantageous for all involved, as cooperation and consultation amongst the trustees facilitates addressing overlapping areas of trustee concern, and consolidates those concerns into a single case. Trustees can also share data, achieve economies of scale, avoid duplication of effort and minimize administrative burdens and expenses. Responsible parties also benefit, as they are able to address trustee concerns in a single, unified case.

The Restoration Program continues to make progress in conducting many of its damage assessment cases on a cooperative basis with responsible parties. As a matter of practice, responsible parties are invited to participate in the development of assessment and restoration plans. The Department has been involved in forty-three cooperative assessments across the nation, where the responsible parties have elected to participate in the damage assessment process, and provide input into the selection of various injury studies and contribute funds for or reimburse Interior assessment activities. In Fiscal Year 2012, nearly $33 million in advanced and/or reimbursed cooperative assessment funding was received from cooperating responsible parties for DOI's assessment activities at twelve sites, including $31.0 million from BP related to the Deepwater Horizon Oil Spill in the Gulf of Mexico. This continuously-focused effort to use

Cooperative Funding and Participation Agreements with responsible parties to the greatest extent possible allows the Department to stretch its discretionary appropriated funds further, thus funding work on additional cases it might not otherwise fund.

Selection of damage assessment projects is accomplished on an annual basis through an extensive internal proposal and screening process that assures that only the highest priority cases are funded. Significant consideration is given to those damage assessment cases that have the potential to address and support Administration or Secretarial priorities and initiatives, such as *America's Great Outdoors* or the *National Blueways System*. Criteria for selecting initial projects are based upon a case's likelihood of success in achieving restoration, either through negotiated restoration settlements or through successful litigation where necessary. Cases must demonstrate sufficient technical, legal, and administrative merit focused on the purpose of achieving restoration.

The Restoration Program's project selection process is designed to:

- Be inclusive of all natural resources under Interior trusteeship and trustee roles;
- Provide a process that encourages thorough planning and ultimately, strong opportunities for restoration success;
- Provide a process that evaluates both the objective and subjective aspects of individual cases; and
- Fund cases that have demonstrated sufficient levels of technical and legal merit, trustee organization, and case readiness.

DOI bureaus are also required to coordinate their efforts into a single project proposal, thus promoting inter-Departmental efficiencies and eliminating duplication of effort. Bureau and DOI office capabilities are used to augment and complement each other, as opposed to building redundant program capabilities in multiple bureaus.

Once projects are funded, the Restoration Program makes use of project-level performance information to inform and guide future funding decisions. The Restoration Program relies on performance data collected from ongoing cases that document the attainment of specific chronological milestones (trustee MOU, assessment plan development, injury determination and quantification, preliminary estimate of damages, etc.) in the multi-year process toward settlement. Funding decisions are weighted in favor of those cases that continue to show progress along the damage assessment continuum towards settlement and eventual restoration. Cases that stall or fail to progress are considered a lesser priority, and are given direction to make course corrections at a stable or reduced funding level. Course corrections must be made before additional funding is made available for addressing future milestones. For example, a case team may be directed to finalize necessary procedural products such as a publicly-announced assessment plan before beginning its scientific studies. The use of such project-level performance data lends itself to helping the Restoration Program better manage its workload by having a clearer sense of when damage assessment cases are near completion and opportunities for new starts emerge.

In addition to project milestone reporting, financial obligation data is monitored at the aggregate (DOI), bureau, and project levels across all involved bureaus. This obligation data and carryover balances are factors considered in the annual funding decision process. Further, unobligated balances on all damage assessment projects are closely monitored from inception through settlement, at which time all unused or unneeded funds are pulled back and re-allocated to other high-priority damage assessment projects. In some instances and under certain circumstances, case teams have been directed to or have voluntarily returned project funds from ongoing projects so that they can be re-allocated to other projects and needs.

The program requires its case teams to document their respective assessment costs and attempts to recover those costs from the potentially responsible parties when negotiating settlement agreements. Over the past three fiscal year funding cycles (2011 – 2013), the Program has utilized an average of $2.1 million annually in damage assessment funds recovered in settlement, in combination with its annual discretionary appropriations in order to continue ongoing damage assessment work at current sites or to initiate new cases.

2014 Activity Performance

In 2014, the program will continue to utilize a mix of discretionary appropriations, recovered past assessment costs from recent settlements and/or returned funds from completed assessments, as well as advanced funds from cooperative responsible parties to meet its damage assessment workload requirements. The combined appropriated and recovered funds will support new or ongoing damage assessment efforts at approximately 30 sites, maintaining the program's damage assessment capability at current levels. This level of funding will support new feasibility studies, initiation of assessments at new sites where warranted, as well as providing continued funding for ongoing cases. As has been the norm in recent years, the program anticipates that the annual project proposals received from the field will exceed the amount of appropriated funding, thus leading the program to select and fund those cases best focused on Administration and Secretarial priorities, and best organized and prepared to advance towards settlement. The program will also continue its focus on the use of cooperative assessments, and pursue advance funding agreements with potentially responsible parties wherever and whenever possible. Money provided under these funding agreements will expand program coverage by allowing other damage assessment cases to utilize the appropriated and recovered/returned assessment funds. In addition, the program will continue to refine its milestone reporting process and use that performance data to enhance management of its damage assessment workload.

The Program's current damage assessment project caseload through 2013 totals 51 ongoing cases (including feasibility studies), and are among those depicted on the map and table on the following pages.

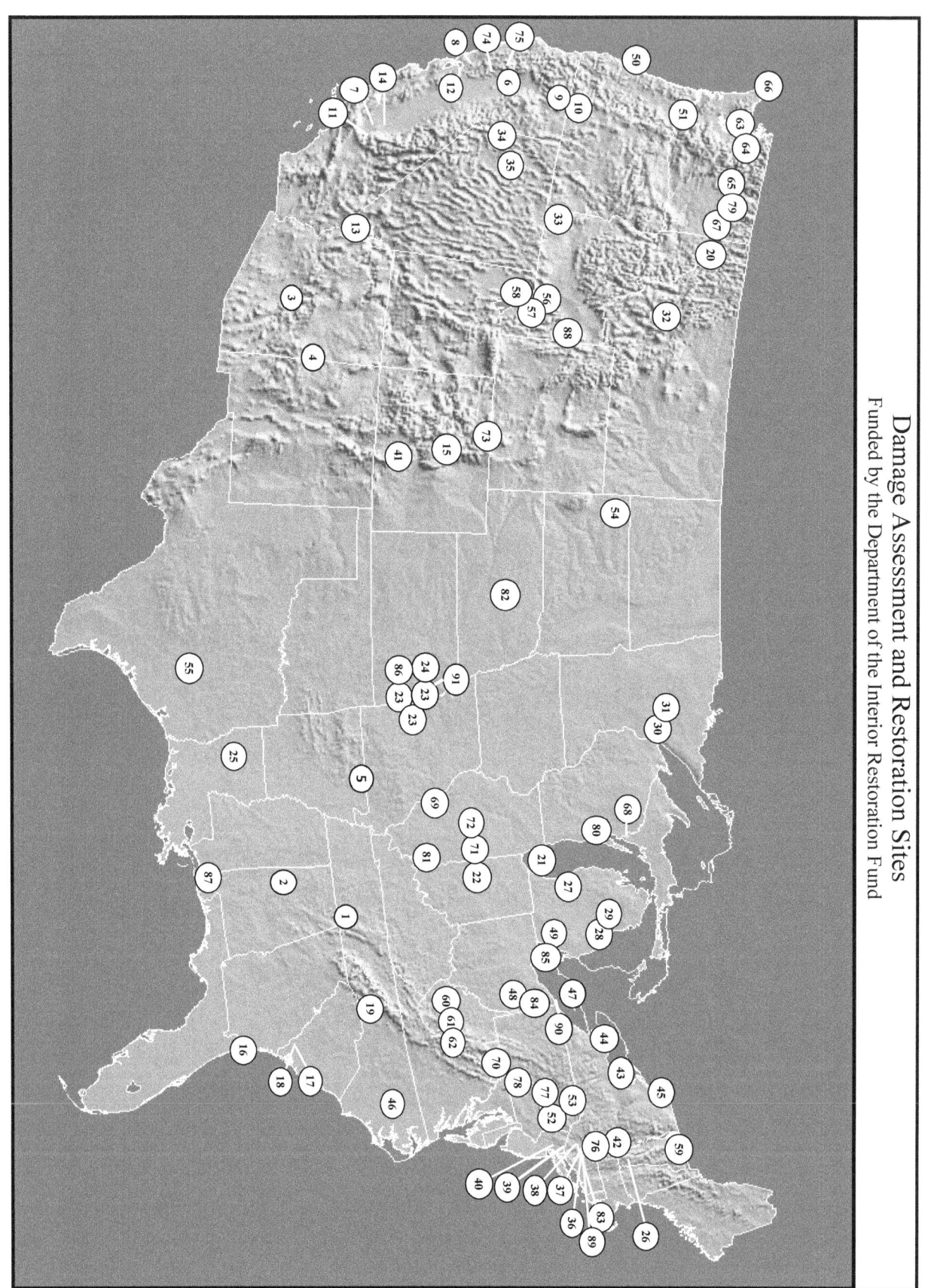

Damage Assessment and Restoration Sites
Funded by the Department of the Interior Restoration Fund

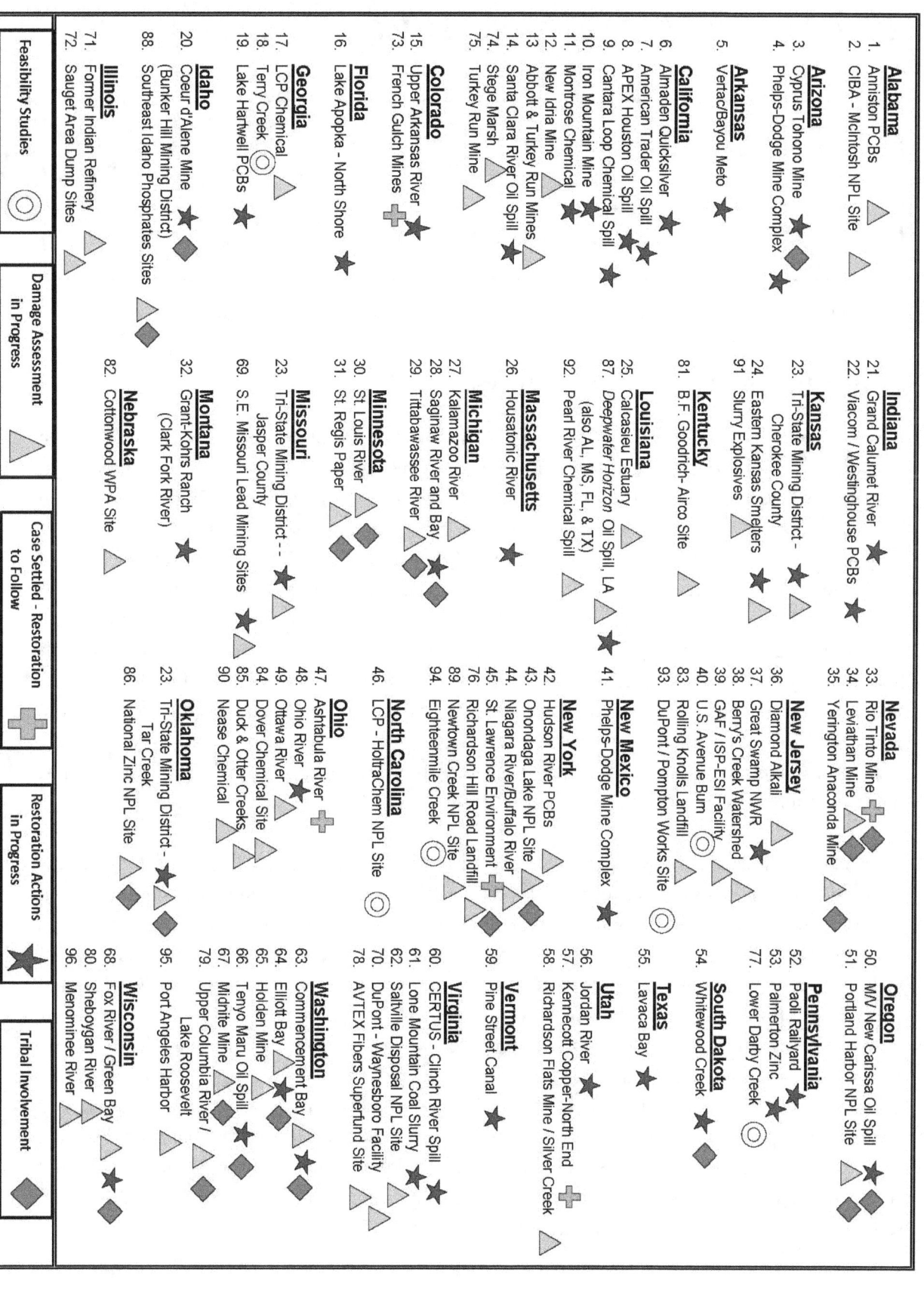

Alabama
1. Anniston PCBs
2. CIBA - McIntosh NPL Site

Arizona
3. Cyprus Tohono Mine
4. Phelps-Dodge Mine Complex

Arkansas
5. Vertac/Bayou Meto

California
6. Almaden Quicksilver
7. American Trader Oil Spill
8. APEX Houston Oil Spill
9. Cantara Loop Chemical Spill
10. Iron Mountain Mine
11. Montrose Chemical
12. New Idria Mine
13. Abbott & Turkey Run Mines
14. Santa Clara River Oil Spill
74. Stege Marsh
75. Turkey Run Mine

Colorado
15. Upper Arkansas River
73. French Gulch Mines

Florida
16. Lake Apopka - North Shore

Georgia
17. LCP Chemical
18. Terry Creek
19. Lake Hartwell PCBs

Idaho
20. Coeur d'Alene Mine
   (Bunker Hill Mining District)
88. Southeast Idaho Phosphates Sites

Illinois
71. Former Indian Refinery
72. Sauget Area Dump Sites

Indiana
21. Grand Calumet River
22. Viacom / Westinghouse PCBs

Kansas
23. Tri-State Mining District -
   Cherokee County
24. Eastern Kansas Smelters
91. Slurry Explosives

Kentucky
81. B.F. Goodrich- Airco Site

Louisiana
25. Calcasieu Estuary
87. *Deepwater Horizon* Oil Spill, LA
   (also AL, MS, FL, & TX)
92. Pearl River Chemical Spill

Massachusetts
26. Housatonic River

Michigan
27. Kalamazoo River
28. Saginaw River and Bay
29. Tittabawassee River

Minnesota
30. St. Louis River
31. St. Regis Paper

Missouri
23. Tri-State Mining District - -
   Jasper County
69. S.E. Missouri Lead Mining Sites

Montana
32. Grant-Kohrs Ranch
   (Clark Fork River)

Nebraska
82. Cottonwood WPA Site

Nevada
33. Rio Tinto Mine
34. Leviathan Mine
35. Yerington Anaconda Mine

New Jersey
36. Diamond Alkali
37. Great Swamp NWR
38. Berry's Creek Watershed
39. GAF / ISP-ESI Facility
40. U.S. Avenue Burn
83. Rolling Knolls Landfill
93. DuPont / Pompton Works Site

New Mexico
41. Phelps-Dodge Mine Complex

New York
42. Hudson River PCBs
43. Onondaga Lake NPL Site
44. Niagara River/Buffalo River
45. St. Lawrence Environment
76. Richardson Hill Road Landfill
89. Newtown Creek NPL Site
94. Eighteenmile Creek

North Carolina
46. LCP - HoltraChem NPL Site

Ohio
47. Ashtabula River
48. Ohio River
49. Ottawa River
84. Dover Chemical Site
85. Duck & Otter Creeks
90. Nease Chemical

Oklahoma
23. Tri-State Mining District -
   Tar Creek
86. National Zinc NPL Site

Oregon
50. M/V New Carissa Oil Spill
51. Portland Harbor NPL Site

Pennsylvania
52. Paoli Railyard
53. Palmerton Zinc
77. Lower Darby Creek

South Dakota
54. Whitewood Creek

Texas
55. Lavaca Bay

Utah
56. Jordan River
57. Kennecott Copper-North End
58. Richardson Flats Mine / Silver Creek

Vermont
59. Pine Street Canal

Virginia
60. CERTUS - Clinch River Spill
61. Lone Mountain Coal Slurry
62. Saltville Disposal NPL Site
70. DuPont - Waynesboro Facility
78. AVTEX Fibers Superfund Site

Washington
63. Commencement Bay
64. Elliott Bay
65. Holden Mine
66. Tenyo Maru Oil Spill
67. Midnite Mine
79. Upper Columbia River /
   Lake Roosevelt
95. Port Angeles Harbor

Wisconsin
68. Fox River / Green Bay
80. Sheboygan River
96. Menominee River

Feasibility Studies ◎
Damage Assessment in Progress ▷
Case Settled - Restoration to Follow ✚
Restoration Actions in Progress ★
Tribal Involvement ◆

23

ACTIVITY: RESTORATION SUPPORT

Appropriation: Natural Resource Damage Assessment		*2013 Full Yr. CR (PL. 112-175)*	2012 Enacted	Fixed Costs	Internal Transfers (+/-)	Program Changes (+/-)	2014 Request
Activity: Restoration Support	$000	*1,160*	613	+9	+570	+3,605	4,797
	FTE	*4*	2	0	0	+9	11

Note: 2012 FTE amounts reflect actual usage, not 2012 enacted formulation estimates.

Justification of 2014 Program Changes:

Restoration Support (+$3,605,000 / +9 FTE) - The 2014 budget request for Restoration Support is $4,797,000 and 11 direct FTE, a program increase of $3,605,000 and 9 direct FTE from the 2012 enacted level. The budget continues the internal transfer of $570,000, initiated in 2013 from the Damage Assessment activity. The requested increase is needed to provide staff support to restoration case managers. The DOI Restoration Fund holds a growing balance of funds recovered in settlements of previous damage assessment cases. Over the last three years, the Fund has received an average of over $150 million per year in restoration settlements and cooperative damage assessment funds, increasing the balance of funds two-fold. A number of long-running damage assessments cases have recently settled, many with multi-million dollar settlements. Still others are in settlement negotiations and are expected to settle soon. At the same time, the Department's current Restoration Program programmatic infrastructure and restoration-focused staffing has not kept pace with this explosive growth in settlement funds. Additional staffing is needed to implement settlement funded restoration.

The requested increase for Restoration Support in 2014 will enable the Department to address growing staffing demands, as current levels inhibit its ability to expeditiously implement additional restoration actions. While bureau-staffed case teams can and do use settlement funds for staff time and to implement on-the-ground restoration actions, there is an absence of dedicated restoration support personnel that are often necessary to successfully plan and implement a restoration plan. For any given settlement, the parties responsible for the spill or release of hazardous substances into the environment are responsible for restoring injured natural resources for that specific site. However, they bear no responsibility for maintaining the necessary cadre of restoration specialists needed to successfully staff and support a wide range of restoration support activities across the Nation. The additional discretionary funding will catalyze the expenditure of settlement funds, by providing scientific, engineering, legal, and contracting support and information exchange nationally, beyond the case-specific scope of the settlement funds recovered from the Responsible Parties.

With the requested increase, the Program's Restoration Support Unit (RSU) would expand its current capacity into a centralized, streamlined "one-stop shop" for restoration implementation. The RSU staff will offer a dedicated skill set which addresses those areas and skills in restoration planning and implementation that have long been identified by field practitioners as being needed to staff case teams to enable timely restoration. The RSU would provide a wide suite of restoration support services to case teams and trustee councils across the Nation, including the following:

- Restoration planning, including development of required restoration plans which must be publicly reviewed;
- Restoration science technical support;
- National Environmental Policy Act (NEPA) compliance support;
- Engineering Support (General engineering, hydrology, fluvial geomorphology, construction engineering, value engineering and cost estimation);
- Project management planning and support, and
- Liaison with other restoration programs and services across the spectrum (government/contractor/non-profits/local organizations)

In addition, the requested 2014 increase would provide for additional staff (as allocation FTE) assigned to the RSU that would provide additional restoration support services, including:

- Legal Support (Office of the Solicitor) to address various restoration-related legal issues, review documents and counsel case teams nationwide;
- Contracting Support (located within a bureau): Dedicated contracting support (with appropriate warrant level), and
- Realty Support (located within a bureau): Services would include coordination of appraisals, title search, contaminants inventory, and other due diligence functions, and coordination of conservation easement processes (baseline inventory, managing oversight, and managing agreements).

Additional restoration support services which could be provided through the RSU may be identified during the program evaluation discussed in ….

By providing dedicated, readily-available restoration support staff, tools, and services, the RSU will seek to supplement and complement the efforts of the bureau-level case teams, who already have the important day-to-day operational and working relationships with other involved co-trustee agencies.

Initially, the RSU will look to jump-start restoration actions at sites where recovered settlement funds have sat idle for more than three years, as well as focus efforts at the largest settlements held in the Restoration Fund.

The potential benefits associated with this budget request are significant, for both injured natural resources and the American public. With nearly a half billion dollars in settlement funds currently residing in the DOI Restoration Fund, and more settlements on the horizon, moving forward deliberately and strategically in the implementation of restoration actions at dozens of sites nationwide will produce benefits, both ecologically and economically.

FY 2013 Program Evaluation - In 2013, the Restoration Program (along with involved DOI bureaus) is launching an evaluation to examine its program infrastructure, operations, and staffing on a Department-wide basis. This analysis will be used to develop a strategic plan that will guide the Department's decisions about how to more effectively support active restoration cases. The Department expects that the additional support will help deal with the growing pool of restoration funds and will result in more timely restoration outcomes. The analysis will seek to identify staffing constraints and process bottlenecks in the course of achieving restoration in coordination with our co-trustee partners. New staff dedicated to restoration support will be added in both the Program's Restoration Support Unit, as well as allocated to bureaus and offices to accelerate restoration activities in accord with this expanding workload. The need for Program restructuring and additional staff resources is further heightened by the anticipated additional funds for ecological restoration from a settlement for natural resource injury in the Deepwater Horizon oil spill and through Restore Act activities in the Gulf region.

Activity Overview:

The restoration of injured natural resources is the sole reason for the existence of the Department's Natural Resource Damage Assessment and Restoration Program. Every action the Restoration Program undertakes is done with the end goal of restoration in mind. Upon the successful conclusion of a damage assessment and upon achieving settlement, Departmental bureaus, working in partnership with other affected State, Federal, tribal and/or foreign co-trustees, use settlement funds to carry out restoration activities. Under this activity, the Program continues its coordinated effort to focus greater attention on restoration activities and to expedite the expenditure of settlement funds to develop and implement restoration plans. The program's Restoration Support Unit (RSU) staff, upon request, provides engineering and ecological/biological support to the Department's case managers/teams, as well as assistance with meeting various legal and regulatory compliance requirements (such as NEPA compliance), identifying possible partnering opportunities, and drafting appropriate documents. In addition, the Program continues to work with the USGS in the field of restoration ecology to develop monitoring protocols to better measure the success and impacts of restoration efforts.

In meeting the statutory and regulatory requirements to restore, replace, or acquire the equivalent of the natural resources that were injured by the release of oil or hazardous materials, these restoration activities encompass a wide variety of projects that support the Department's mission of protecting natural and cultural resources. By working with the co-trustees on restoration activities, the Program is able to direct funds that contribute to the President's *America's Great Outdoors* initiative through ecological restoration, land acquisition and/or protection, as well as provide secondary support to the Secretary's *Strengthening Tribal Nations* initiative via tribal co-trustee interactions. In addition, many projects engage youth in restoration activities and outdoor classrooms. These activities include multiple sites in high priority landscapes such as the Great Lakes, the California Bay/Delta, Chesapeake Bay, and the Gulf of Mexico; land acquisition for several National Wildlife Refuges and numerous State and local parks; protection and reintroduction of threatened and endangered species helping lead to their eventual recovery; and protection and restoration of essential habitat for migratory birds and fish.

Over ninety percent of all funds received and interest currently in the Restoration Fund from settled damage assessment cases are designated as restoration funds, and can be used only for restoration planning, implementation (including land acquisition), oversight, and monitoring of implemented restoration actions at a specific site or related to a specific settlement, and only after the issuance of an publicly-reviewed restoration plan. The use of such settlement funds provides real value to the American public, as injured natural resources and services are restored by, or at the expense of the responsible party, and not the taxpaying public.

Other Available Restoration Resources (Dollars in $000)		
	2012	2013
Settlement funds currently held in DOI Restoration Fund (estimate)	$461,632	$465,000
Settlement funds in various court registry accounts (estimate)	$100,000	$100,000

In addition to settlement funds deposited into the DOI Restoration Fund, the Department is party to other natural resource damage settlements where settlement funds are deposited into a Court Registry or some other account selected by the Trustees. Additionally, there are a number of settlements where the responsible parties have agreed to undertake or implement the restoration actions, with trustee agencies providing oversight to ensure compliance with the terms of the settlement and adherence to the approved and public-reviewed restoration plan. Once fully implemented, the restoration actions are then subject to long-term monitoring by the trustees to ensure they have been effective and have met the goals and intent of the restoration plans.

All restoration activities are focused on restoring those resources and the services they provide back to the baseline level they would have had in the absence of the spill or release of hazardous substances. This encompasses preserving and maintaining the lands, waters, and wildlife of the Nation's public lands, embodied in wildlife refuges, national parks, and BLM lands as well as recovering trust resources that are on private and tribal trust lands. Results are achieved through DOI-administered programs and through partnership efforts and in collaboration with others in and out of government. These efforts are as widely varied as the trust resources the Department manages. Examples of these activities include:

- Restoration of nesting habitat for migratory birds;
- Re-introduction and re-establishment of endangered species;
- Acquisition of property that is added to the National Wildlife Refuge System or the lands managed by state, tribal, or local governments;
- In-stream and riparian habitat improvement to improve aquatic communities, fisheries, or fish passage;
- Control or removal of invasive species of plants and animals and re-establishment of native flora and fauna, and
- Providing recreational opportunities or protecting cultural uses and activities that flow from trust resources.

2014 Activity Performance:

Upon completion of the detailed programmatic analysis and development of a strategic plan in late summer of 2013, the Department will begin to implement the strategic plan to markedly increase the amount of restoration implementation across the country, and to effectively utilize the growing balance of restoration settlement funds in the DOI Restoration Fund. An increase in the number of staff dedicated exclusively on implementing restoration will result in significant increases in the amount of acres and stream/shoreline miles being restored

In 2014, the Program will continue to focus its activities in support of trust resource restoration, and will, through the addition of additional Restoration Support staffing and resources, and the implementation of a program strategic plan, see increased restoration outputs and outcomes. Fiscal Year 2014 planned performance targets include the restoration of 22,500 acres and 180 stream or shoreline miles, increases of 3,750 acres (+20%) and 15 stream / shoreline miles (+9%), respectively over FY 2013 strategic plan goals. Attainment of these goals will be accomplished by the Department and its co-trustees through the use of funds or in-kind services received in settlement of damage claims with responsible parties.

In addition to these activities, RSU staff will lead technology transfer and outreach activities to ensure that restoration advances made by individual case teams will be shared with fellow restoration practitioners. Examples include development of restoration training modules to be taught at the FWS and BLM training centers, and the organization of seminar sessions at the Restoration Program's biennial workshop, and shared through external conduits such as the Society of Environmental Toxicology and Chemistry (SETAC). The RSU will also continue to maintain its partnership with the Society for Ecological Restoration (SER) to develop and maintain an inventory of restoration plans, opportunities, and success stories, as well as the development and implementation of policies and guidance to coordinate NRD restoration planning and NEPA compliance actions.

The RSU will continue to work with the U.S. Geological Survey (USGS) to implement restoration science advances. Scientists from the USGS are working with the Restoration Support Unit in developing protocols to improve the monitoring and management of restoration processes and the development of effective measures of restoration success on historically contaminated lands. Because ecosystems are dynamic, restoration monitoring protocols must serve as triggers for corrective actions and adaptive management and be carefully crafted into restoration plans. USGS and the RSU are working with restoration scientists in the public and private sector to develop a primer for restoration monitoring that will provide the guidance necessary to ensure successful restorations and return ecosystem services to injured resources. These efforts are focusing on species distributions, abundance and diversity, invasive species, community development and, when possible, ecosystem resiliency which is critically important as the NRDAR program addresses the influence of global climate change on restoration planning, the role of global climate change in environmental responses to chemical exposure, how climate change may affect the damage assessment process, and to explore how restoration activities may aid in the adaptation and mitigation of climate change effects in our environment.

USGS and the Restoration Support Unit are also working with the Society for Ecological Restoration (SER) to revise the SER restoration guidelines and to highlight Departmental restoration projects on the SER Global Restoration Network website (http://www.globalrestorationnetwork.org/), a freely accessible internet-based platform where practitioners as well as stakeholders and the general public can go to obtain extensive information on restoration successes and lessons learned in the process. By documenting restoration activities and their ultimate success, the Program can maintain transparency in the process that returns ecosystem services lost as a result of chemical contamination.

These efforts bring USGS science expertise to address the ecological restoration of species and habitats injured by the release of oil or other hazardous substances and the monitoring and measurement of restoration success. Although many scientifically valid techniques are available to document the extent and severity of injury to natural resources, restoration science is still in its infancy. Several interconnected efforts, engaging multiple disciplines within USGS, are being undertaken to strengthen the state of restoration science, reduce disagreements with responsible parties, and help us achieve more timely and effective restoration.

RESTORING INJURED RESOURCES

The following are examples of recent on-the-ground restoration accomplishments achieved by the Department of the Interior's bureaus and their co-trustees at a number of selected sites:

Holyoke Coal Tar Site, Massachusetts

Removal of the first stone from the Bartlett Rod Shop Company Dam on Amethyst Brook, a tributary of Fort River, on October 2012, in Pelham, Massachusetts. Removal of the stone masonry dam will restore passage to nine miles of upstream riverine habitat to migratory fish, benefitting sea lamprey, American eel, brook trout, brown trout and slimy sculpin in the larger Connecticut River watershed. (Photo credit: Meagan Racey, FWS)

The Holyoke Gas Works facility operated from 1852 to 1952 on the west bank of the Connecticut River in Holyoke, Massachusetts, producing coal and petroleum. At least 120,000 gallons of coal tar wastes were released from the plant into the Connecticut River between 1905 and 1952. These coal tar wastes contaminated adjacent soils, groundwater, sediments and surface waters causing injury to fish, including federally-endangered shortnose sturgeon.

The Natural Resource Damages Trustee Council, comprised of representatives from the U.S. Department of the Interior (through the Fish and Wildlife Service), Massachusetts Department of Environmental Protection, and the National Oceanic and Atmospheric Administration settled natural resource damage claims at the Site with Holyoke Water Power Co. and the City of Holyoke Gas & Electric Department, successors to the responsible parties. The settlement provided $345,000 for natural resource restoration project planning, implementation and administration. With accrued interest, the restoration fund grew to $395,000.

In May 2012 the trustees released a publicly-reviewed Final Restoration Plan selecting three projects to restore injured natural resources and natural resource services they provide to the public such as enhanced recreational fishing and improved water quality. The trustees allocated funds to; 1) remove the now-defunct Bartlett Rod Shop Company Dam in Pelham; 2) complete construction of the Manhan River fishway in Easthampton, and 3) monitor rare freshwater mussels in the Connecticut River and its tributaries.

The Bartlett Rod Shop Company Dam on Amethyst Brook, a tributary of the Connecticut River, was removed in October 2012. Removal of the stone masonry dam restored upstream riverine habitat to migratory fish, benefitting the American eel, sea lamprey, brook trout, brown trout and slimy sculpin in the larger Connecticut River watershed. A remnant portion of the dam was left intact to commemorate the dam's 192-year history. Dam removal projects such as this can help restore fisheries by opening up fish access to critical spawning and rearing habitat; allow sediment transport to nourish downstream habitats; improve water quality; and increase opportunities for recreational and commercial fishing interests.

Partially completed Manhan River dam fishway in Easthampton, MA. Settlement funds from the Holyoke Gas Tar Deposits settlement contribute to the overall funds needed to complete the Denil fishway for anadromous fish passage. (Photo credit: FWS)

The second project involves the construction of a fish ladder on the Manhan River dam. The project is expected to be completed by the end of the summer 2013. This project will reopen over

10 miles of spawning and nursery habitat along the river and its main tributary for resident fish, as well as for blueback herring, Atlantic salmon, American shad, sea lamprey and American eel. The Manhan Dam project design includes a viewing window and remote monitoring equipment (video camera with post-processing software to speed up fish counts) to track the movement of fish past the dam to the newly-opened habitat. The USGS is assisting with the equipment/system set up. The City will work with a local environmental group to ensure several years of follow-up monitoring at the site.

The third project is expected to begin in the summer of 2013, as crews survey and monitor rare freshwater mussels in the Connecticut River and its tributaries. The 410-mile long Connecticut River and its 7.2 million acre watershed is the first river designated as a National Blueway, and these restoration projects will contribute to the enhancement of water quality, fish passage, and recreational opportunities.

Montrose Chemical Superfund Site / American Trader Oil Spill, CA
Channel Islands, California

From the late 1940s through the early 1970s, millions of pounds of dichlorodiphenyltrichloroethane (DDT) and polychlorinated biphenyls (PCBs) were discharged from industrial sources through a wastewater outfall into the ocean at White Point, near Los Angeles. Large quantities of these chemicals remain and continue to harm birds and fishing in the area. In 2000, the final settlement was signed, ending ten years of litigation. Approximately $30 million of this settlement was available for restoration to address the natural resource injuries and the public's lost use of resources.

The nearby Channel Islands are home to plants and animals found nowhere else on Earth. This includes 145 endemic or unique species. The Montrose Trustee Council (Department of the Interior, through the Fish and Wildlife Service and National Park Service, NOAA, and the State of California) have pursued a number of important eagle and seabird restoration projects which were enhanced in the Channel Islands National Park, using funding from the Montrose Settlement Restoration Program (MSRP). These projects are crucially important for burrow-nesting seabirds, which are threatened by habitat loss, non-native predators, and changing ocean conditions.

A project to counter the negative impacts of feral cats on marine birds and other native wildlife was recently completed on Navy-owned San Nicolas Island, located 61 miles due west of Los Angeles. The island is 23 square miles in area and the most remote of the eight islands in the Channel Island Archipelago. The island provides vital nesting habitat for native seabirds and shorebirds. It boasts numerous other wildlife, including the endemic San Nicolas island fox, the island night lizard, and breeding seals and sea lions. Cats, first brought to the island in the 1950's, have preyed on the island's nesting seabirds and shorebirds and competed with other endemic species on the island. Removal of the non-native feral cats is intended to benefit the ground-nesting seabirds and shorebirds. In 2009, the MSRP partnered with the U.S. Navy, Island Conservation, the Institute for Wildlife Studies, and the Humane Society of the United States to completely remove the feral cats from San Nicolas Island. The project humanely relocated 59 adult cats and 10 kittens from the island to the Humane Society of the United States. The removal of the feral cats boosted fox, night lizard, seabird, and shorebird populations. In 2012, after two years of extensive monitoring San Nicolas Island was declared cat free.

Phase 1 of the seabird restoration work continued on Santa Barbara Island, within Channel Islands National Park, by adding 6 acres of Cassin's auklet and Scripps's murrelet nesting habitat by both expanding existing plant restoration sites and adding new areas. The Scripps murrelet is among the world's rarest seabirds. Restoration work consisted of removing non-native vegetation and planting native plants that are cultivated on the island. Biologists also encouraged nesting in the restored areas by using social attraction and deploying nest boxes in order to facilitate monitoring efforts.

At Scorpion Rock, located off Santa Cruz Island within Channel Islands National Park, the goal was to restore an additional acre of habitat for the Cassin's auklet, ashy storm-petrel, and other nesting seabirds. This project was a continuation and expansion of the restoration work begun on Scorpion Rock in Phase 1. Restoration efforts undertaken during Phase 1 established numerous native plants on the rock and reduced percent cover of non-native vegetation, principally iceplant. Despite aggressive efforts to remove iceplant, continued effort is needed to restore Scorpion Rock until the native plants are fully established and can out-compete the iceplant and other exotic vegetation.

A rare Scripp's murrelet is shown in a sea cave nest on Anacapa Island in Channel Islands National Park, offshore southern California. Since the 2001 – 2002 eradication of exotic black rats from the island, the number of Scripp's murrelet nests on Anacapa Island has quadrupled and hatching success has increased. (Photo credit: Sarah Thomsen, NPS)

Habitat restoration work continued with additional exotic vegetation removal, native plant re-vegetation, enhancing the nest boxes used by the Cassin's auklets, and monitoring their reproductive success. The removal of exotic vegetation and the planting of native plants on Santa Barbara Island and on Scorpion Rock were conducted during the non-breeding season to avoid impacts to nesting birds.

Restoring the natural balance of island ecosystems through the removal of non-native species has been shown to have significant positive effects. To restore balance to Anacapa Island's ecosystem, non-native black rats were removed in 2001 and 2002 using an aerial application of rodenticide bait. The $1.5 million project was funded through settlement of the 1990 *T/V American Trader* oil spill offshore Huntington Beach, California. Ten years after removing the non-native black rats from the ecosystem on Anacapa Island, many species, including rare seabirds, are showing profound results of recovery. Ashy storm-petrels are nesting on the island for the first time ever recorded, and Cassin's auklets have expanded their territories in the absence of rats as predators. Most significantly, the number of Scripps's murrelet nests has quadrupled with a 50 percent increase of eggs hatched.

Westinghouse PCB NPL Sites, Indiana

From 1958 to 1972, CBS (formerly Westinghouse Electric Corp.) operated a plant in Bloomington, Indiana, where it manufactured electrical capacitors containing an insulating fluid composed of polychlorinated biphenyls (PCBs). CBS disposed of defective capacitors at 8 local dumps and landfills, and released PCBs from its plant through the sewer system. It wasn't until the late 1970s that harmful levels of PCBs were detected in streams, sediments, plants, and wildlife around the Bloomington area.

A 1984 consent decree mandating the construction of an incinerator to burn excavated PCB-contaminated soil and sewage sludge received public opposition and was subsequently amended in 2009. An amended consent decree specified alternative remedial actions for Lemon Lane

Bobcat cubs recently observed on the Columbia Mine Tract at Patoka River National Wildlife Refuge.
Photo credit: Steve Gifford

Landfill, Neal's Landfill, and Bennett's Dump Superfund sites, and awarded $1.88 million in settlement to the Department of the Interior, acting through the Fish and Wildlife Service (FWS), as compensation for natural resource injuries to migratory birds and endangered bats, as well as a portion of past assessment costs. The amended decree also specified settlement funds be used by the Department to conduct or finance projects to permanently protect and restore riparian and forested wetland habitat in the White River/Patoka River watershed.

River otters recently observed on the Columbia Mine tract at the Patoka River National Wildlife Refuge. The tract was acquired using settlement funds from a natural resource damages settlement. (Photo credit: Steve Gifford)

In September 2012, the Department of the Interior, through the FWS, acquired the management rights to 1,043 acres known as the Columbia Mine Tract, which was then incorporated into the Patoka River National Wildlife Refuge, located in Pike and Gibson Counties in southwestern Indiana. This parcel of land was purchased with $1.1 million from the Westinghouse settlement fund. The specific habitats on the Columbia Mine Tract include 350 acres of upland mixed forest and grassland, 245 acres of grassland/savannah, 89 acres of open water marsh and river channels, 359 acres of palustrine scrub/shrub and forested wetlands, and 13 miles of lakeshore, oxbow and river channel riparian habitat. With this addition, the Patoka River NWR now totals 8,007 acres. This acquisition completes an area called Snakey Point Marsh.

The Patoka River NWR has been listed by the National Audubon Society as an Important Bird Area because it contains large breeding populations of many declining species. Birds of interest in the Snakey Point area include bald eagle (nesting), cerulean warbler, Acadian flycatcher, red-headed woodpecker, pileated woodpecker, red-shouldered hawk, prothonotary warbler, Henslow sparrow, and grasshopper sparrow. In addition, Northern shrike, rough-legged hawk, shorteared owls and northern harrier are commonly seen using the area and a Mississippi kite was also observed recently. Federally endangered Indiana bats use this area for summer maternity trees. Bobcats and river otters, both species reintroduced in Indiana, have been recently observed on the Columbia Mine Tract, and the state endangered swamp rabbit is also a likely resident. A natural population of the threatened northern copperbelly water snake is also present in the area. This site is now managed to meet the objectives of the Patoka River NWR Comprehensive Conservation Plan. The plan directs the protection of this area, one of the most significant bottomland hardwood forests remaining in the Midwest.

M/V Stuyvesant & M/V Kure Oil Spills, California

In 1997 the container ship *M/V Kure* ruptured its hull while docking and spilled approximately 4,500 gallons of bunker fuel oil into Humboldt Bay, California. Then in 1999, the Dredge *M/V Stuyvesant* ruptured its hull with a dredge arm during dredging operations and caused a spill of at least 2,100 gallons of bunker fuel oil into the Pacific Ocean near the mouth of Humboldt Bay. In both cases the oil dispersed along the outer coastline, mainly north of the bay. The expanse of the spilled oil reached from the mouth of the Eel River to Patrick's Point State Park, roughly 18 miles.

Both spills impacted natural resources under the trusteeship of Federal and State trustees, the Department of the Interior and the State of California. The trustees for the *M/V Kure* settled the Natural Resource Damage Assessment (NRDA) portion of the case for $4.82 million. This included $2.42 million for various habitat and recreational use projects, and a conservation easement for the E.F. Hunter and Big Mynot forest parcels located in the lower Klamath basin, valued at $2.4 million. From the *M/V Stuyvesant* spill, trustees settled the NRDA portion of the case for $6.71 million. This included over $2 million for various habitat and recreational use projects, and a conservation easement for the Miracle Mile forest parcel, valued at over $4 million including monitoring costs. The settlement monies from these two spills, both near Humboldt Bay along the northern shore of California, were used to fund joint restoration projects in order to maximize benefits on behalf of the public.

The Humboldt Bay water complex is the fifth largest estuary on the West Coast and second largest in California. The Bay includes an extensive system of tidal mudflats and eelgrass beds that provide diverse fish and macro invertebrate communities, as well as highly productive year-round foraging habitats for wading birds and shorebirds. Humboldt Bay also provides important habitat as a wintering and migratory staging area to shorebirds.

The Mike Thompson South Spit Humboldt Bay Wildlife Area is a 4.4 mile long, mostly sandy stretch of land that separates the southern portion of Humboldt Bay from the Pacific Ocean. Funding for several restoration projects was provided through the *Stuyvesant-Kure* oil spill settlement funds for continued restoration and maintenance activities at South Spit, including enhancement of the nesting area for the threatened western snowy plover. The nesting habitat enhancement effort included oyster shell placement, vegetation management, predator deterrence, and feral cat trapping. Since the Department of the Interior (through the Bureau of Land Management (BLM)) has managed South Spit, approximately 51 acres of beach habitat has been re-contoured and cleared of European beachgrass to facilitate breeding. To increase nesting activity and nest success rates, 600 cubic yards of oyster shells covering 10.5 acres were applied to South Spit. The oyster shells provide cover for snowy plovers and their eggs.

South Spit's 800 acres are home to numerous animal species throughout the year, including a small resident herd of black-tailed deer, striped skunks, gray fox, short-tailed weasels, ground squirrels, raccoons, feral cats, song birds, shorebirds, raptors, and ravens. While most of the vegetation is dominated by non-native species such as European beachgrass, the BLM has been steadily restoring the dunes. The restoration effort requires multiple treatments of the same area. The main benefactors of this restoration effort have been the federally endangered plants Humboldt Bay wallflower and beach layia.

Western snowy plovers, a threatened species benefitting from M/V Kure and M/V Stuyvesant oil spills restoration actions in Humboldt County, CA. (FWS photo)

At nearby Little River State Beach, state co-trustees California Department of Fish and Wildlife and the California State Parks have embarked upon a similar restoration effort, using *Stuyvesant-*

Kure settlement funds to implement restoration projects aimed at restoring the ecological function and the native flora and fauna found within approximately 40 acres of nearshore dunes by addressing the spread of invasive European beachgrass and yellow bush lupine, which have steadily displaced native plant communities and contributed to the loss and degradation of nearshore dunes habitat. Second, the project sought to enhance breeding and sheltering habitat for the threatened western snowy plover, as the beach is part of one of the few remaining active breeding sites for snowy plovers in Humboldt County. Implementation began 2009, and most of the project's objectives (invasive eradication and re-vegetation with native species) have been accomplished. In addition, the average number of snowy western plovers wintering on the beach has steadily increased since 2010 when a large portion of the nearshore dune restoration was completed.

ACTIVITY: ONSHORE OIL SPILL PREPAREDNESS

Oiled Canada geese at the Marshall River Pipeline Spill, MI (FWS Photo)

Appropriation: Natural Resource Damage Assessment	2013 Full Yr. CR (PL. 112-175)	2012 Enacted	Fixed Costs	Internal Transfers (+/-)	Program Changes (+/-)	2014 Request
Activity: Onshore Oil Spill Preparedness	0	0	0	0	+2,200	2,200
FTE	0	0	0	0	+2	2

Note: FY2012 FTE reflects actual usage.

Justification of 2014 Program Changes:

Onshore Oil Spill Preparedness ($2,200,000 / +2 FTE) - The 2014 budget request for Oil Spill Preparedness is $2,200,000 and 2 FTE, a program increase of $2,200,000 and 2 FTE from the 2012 enacted level. Conventional energy resources will continue to remain an important component as the Department moves forward in implementing the New Energy Frontier Initiative. Domestic oil and gas production and transportation are likely to continue at high, and potentially increasing, levels. The new forms of transportation beginning to enter into the industry (e.g., tank cars on high-speed rail and pipelines carrying tar sands/bitumen oil) pose new risks and challenges to planners and responders. While other government programs and industry partners are focused on improving efficiencies and safeguards, accidents could still occur and the Department must be better prepared to respond to oil spills that occur onshore. An effective, timely response results in an overall reduction in the cost of responding to a spill, reduces the extent of injuries to trust resources, and impacts to the environment and people.

In 2014, the Department is requesting funds to improve its onshore oil spill response readiness. The funds would be used to train employees in onshore spill preparedness, including understanding response techniques, participation in contingency planning, and establishing and maintaining an operational program that will result in more timely and more effective Departmental response to future onshore oil spills.

This proposal addresses a recommendation from the National Commission on the Deepwater Horizon Oil Spill and Offshore Drilling that the Department "...should create a rigorous, transparent, and meaningful oil spill risk analysis and planning process for the development and implementation of better oil spill response."

Activity Overview:

Through the National Response System, EPA leads the federal response for inland oil spills and the U.S. Coast Guard leads the federal response for offshore and navigable waterways, including major rivers, lakes and bays. DOI is the primary Federal natural resource trustee with vast resources threatened by oil spills, including recreational areas and commercially valuable resources. It is critical that DOI serve as a strong partner in the oil spill contingency planning process and have internal capacity to do so.

Discharges of oil and other hazardous substances from production of petroleum products, transportation, and onshore facilities, including pipelines, can injure trust resources in a variety of ways. The Secretary of the Interior has trust responsibility for resources such as threatened and endangered species, national wildlife refuges, national parks, monuments, seashores, and historic sites, national conservation lands, reservoirs, allotted water rights, and certain Indian lands. When a spill occurs, employees of the Department's many Bureaus are often the first responders, along with State employees and EPA. Pre-incident planning requires DOI employees to participate in local, regional and national contingency planning including contingency response teams, area contingency plans and exercises for spill responses. It is this participation that results in effective teamwork when there is a spill incident. In addition, the Department's Incident Qualification and Classification and Resource Ordering Systems provide critical support to oil spill incident responses. To highlight this first response, in 2012 alone, DOI employees responded to over 900 incidents nationwide.

The pilot program's objective is to improve DOI's overall preparedness for potential inland oil spills in ways that can better protect the Nation's natural and cultural resources, historic properties, and DOI lands, resources, and interests. The pilot program is a coordinated, integrated, cross-cutting effort involving FWS, NPS, USGS, BLM, BIA, BOR, the Office of

Environmental Policy and Compliance (OEPC), and the Office of Emergency Management (OEM) that will identify and support targeted work on Regional, Area, and Geographic Contingency Plans based on where the greatest risks and vulnerabilities exist that might adversely affect DOI lands, resources, and interests. Strong DOI engagement in the planning process is critical because these plans establish the response strategies that will be put into effect by initial responders during the first few hours of an oil spill.

Oil spill response actions at the March 2013 derailment of a Canadian Pacific Railroad train transporting crude oil from Canada. The derailment, near Parkers Prairie in northwest Minnesota, leaked an estimated 15,000 gallons. (Photo credit: Doug Bellefeuille, Minnesota Pollution Control Agency)

One focal point of the pilot program is improving inland oil spill preparedness through work on Regional, Area and Geographic Contingency Plans according to where the greatest risks and vulnerabilities exist that may adversely affect DOI lands, resources, and interests. These risks include proximity to:

- Oil and Gas Pipelines
- Oil and Gas Production areas
- Fuel Truck Transportation Routes
- Rail Transport of Petroleum Products
- Oil, Gas and Chemical Refining, Manufacturing and Storage Complexes

There has been a rapid increase in rail transport of crude in the last three years as new drilling technologies in North America have unlocked vast reserves of oil previously deemed too expensive to extract, although crude still represents a small fraction of U.S. rail transport. U.S. trains carried 233,800 carloads of crude oil in 2012, more than triple the 65,800 carloads transported in 2011 and dwarfing the 29,600 in 2010, according to figures from the Association of American Railroads.

As transportation of crude oil by rail has increased in the United States, so have spill incidents. Of the 132 incidents that occurred while trains were in transit in the United States between 2002 and 2012, 112 occurred in the last three years, according to data from the Pipeline and Hazardous Materials Safety Administration.

OEPC leads and coordinates DOI's participation in the National Response System for both preparedness and response. One of its key activities is to coordinate DOI input to the Area Committee planning process, but DOI bureaus' budget constraints have limited their participation. While OEPC can provide generalized information regarding DOI resources, field-level and resource-specific expertise from the Bureaus is needed to identify specific areas for oil collection and deflection, as well avoidance areas for personnel and equipment. Resource constraints and competing priorities to date have limited DOI's involvement in broad EPA and USCG-led activities. The proposed increase will expand participation by DOI bureaus in EPA and USCG-led Area Committee meetings and exercises will result in: (1) more accurate information on DOI trust resources in Area Contingency Plans, (2) improved notification and communication between EPA/USCG and DOI during oil spill responses, and (3) more familiarity by DOI resource managers with oil spill response operations and organizations. The pilot project will fund DOI Bureau oil spill responders and land/resource managers' participation in Area Committee planning and preparedness activities, enabling them to work with EPA and USCG On-Scene Coordinators who subsequently manage oil spill responses that affect DOI trust resources, inform Area Committees about local DOI trust resources, and ensure necessary environmental safeguards are adopted in Area Contingency Plans.

In addition, the pilot program will support DOI Bureau field staff's participation in Area Committee oil spill response exercises alongside EPA and USCG staff, to experience and learn oil spill response organizations and operations, the role of the RRT, and build necessary relationships to work effectively towards protecting DOI trust resources when an oil spill occurs.

Additional elements of the pilot program would include:

- Establishing a formal interagency preparedness program for pipelines on DOI lands with DOT's Pipeline Hazards Safety Materials Administration (PHMSA), EPA, and specific Regional Response Teams;

- Establishing similar preparedness programs for rail and highway fuel transportation networks with the appropriate DOT counterparts (such as the Federal Railroad Administration), EPA and Regional Response Teams;

- Designing, organizing, and conducting inland oil spill exercises on or near DOI lands;

- Developing an online library of applicable guidance, templates, and technical resources related to contingency planning and response.

- Developing a records system for reporting and tracking spills that DOI responds to, enabling a feedback loop to better prepare for future spills through better sharing of data and information from previous spills;

- Developing and delivering targeted training to support effective engagement in inland oil spill contingency planning and response activities.

2014 Activity Performance:

The pilot program's performance would be evaluated and documented to support recommendations to improve DOI's response preparedness in crosscutting programs, with the Environmental Safeguards Group used to support the pilot program, provide advice, and document its activities.

The DOI Office of Environmental Policy and Compliance (OEPC) will work with DOI bureaus/offices to design the one year pilot program to undertake tangible, specific products and activities that can improve DOI's inland oil spill preparedness. It is important to avoid having each bureau/office pursue its own pilot program independently with no coordination or leveraged efforts. By working together, DOI bureaus and offices can leverage efforts to optimize this pilot program's performance.

The pilot program would identify and support the preparedness participation of field and regional contacts to bolster information in these plans regarding natural and cultural resources, historic properties, and DOI lands, resources, and interests which would likely be threatened by an inland oil spill. This information would be developed and updated using GIS to consolidate data from all of the DOI bureaus/offices and other federal agencies such as EPA and DOT's Pipeline Hazards Safety Materials Administration (PHMSA).

In priority order, the DOI pilot program would:

1. Provide resources to promote DOI bureau/office participation in Area Committee planning activities;

2. Provide resources to promote DOI bureau/office participation in Area Committee oil spill response exercises held by EPA, US Coast Guard (USCG), and Regional Response Teams (RRTs);

3. Develop an interagency inland oil spill preparedness pilot program (or activities) with DOT's Pipeline Hazards Safety Materials Administration (PHMSA), EPA and RRTs;

4. Provide resources to design, organize, and conduct oil spill exercises on DOI lands with the active participation of DOI bureaus, EPA, and RRTs.

5. Develop an online library of applicable guidance, templates, and technical resources related to contingency planning and response; and

6. Develop and deliver targeted training to support effective engagement in inland oil spill contingency planning and response activities, with a special emphasis on highlighting protective measures for tribal lands and cultural resources.

ACTIVITY: PROGRAM MANAGEMENT

Appropriation: Natural Resource Damage Assessment		2013 Full Yr. CR (PL. 112-175)	2012 Enacted	Fixed Costs	Internal Transfers (+/-)	Program Changes (+/-)	2014 Request
Activity: Program Management	$000	1,954	1,903	+197	0	+251	2,351
	FTE	7	7	0	0	0	7

Note: FY2012 FTE reflects actual usage.

Justification of 2014 Program Changes:

Program Management ($251,000) - The 2014 budget request for Program Management is $2,351,000 and 7 direct FTE, a program increase of $251,000 from the 2012 enacted level. The increase will be used to provide a fuller level of funding for the bureau support positions (Restoration Program Workgroup) in the five trustee bureaus (BIA, BLM, BR, FWS, and NPS), and those bureaus and offices providing technical support to the Departmental program. The Program currently provides $85,000 and 0.6 allocation FTE to each participating bureau and office for workgroup participation and program support. As the Program has continued to grow (in terms of settlements and restoration workload), it is vital to provide workgroup funding commensurate with the growing workload. As the Restoration Program begins to implement changes from its programmatic evaluation and subsequent strategic plan, changes to program infrastructure and operations will likely result. The additional funds will be used by the workgroup to carry out these program changes and convey policy and operational requirements through their respective bureau to maximize restoration outcomes

Activity Overview:

Program Management provides the strategic vision, direction, management, and coordination of inter-Departmental activities necessary for the Department to carry out the Restoration Program. In short, it manages the intersection of complex interdisciplinary relationships among biology, environmental toxicology, natural resource management, economics, and law. The Program Management activity allocates damage assessment project funding; monitors program performance and ensures accountability; provides the framework for identifying and resolving issues that raise significant management or policy implications; develops the Department's policies and regulations for conducting and managing damage assessment and restoration cases; responds to Departmental, Executive Office of the President, and Congressional inquiries; and ensures coordination among Federal, State, and tribal governments.

Program Management funding enables the program to maintain support for bureau workgroup representation, ensuring essential integrated program coordination across the Department. The request includes funds for program support positions in the five bureaus with primary trust resource management roles and for technical support offices (USGS, Office of Policy Analysis, and the Office of the Solicitor). A fully integrated Departmental program requires a significant level of bureau participation on the workgroup and Program Management Team, as well as continued regional coordination and technical support in science, economics, and law.

In 2014, the Program Office will continue its ongoing efforts to enhance its outreach to Tribes in two significant ways. First, it continues its monthly conference calls with any tribal co-trustees that have an interest in the natural resources and restoration activities of the Department. Secondly, the program has begun a tribal training initiative where it is partnering with the interested tribal co-trustees to design natural resource damage assessment (NRDA) training for tribal members and technical consultants. This effort will attempt to utilize existing Departmental and tribal training resources, educators and experts to develop a curriculum and materials that are targeted to tribal resources in a NRDA context. Coincident to the Program improving relationships with tribal co-trustees and governments will be an equally ambitious effort to maintain and improve communications with State co-trustees through the continued implementation of a Memorandum of Understanding (MOU) with the Association of Fish & Wildlife Agencies (AFWA). The AFWA MOU will facilitate communications between the Program and the State co-trustee on issues of mutual interest, likely leading to the development of policies, improved assessment techniques and sharing of best practices, and if needed, regulatory revisions.

The Department entered into a Memorandum of Understanding (MOU) with the International Group of Protection and Indemnity Clubs (P&I Clubs) in 2012 to agree to consider appropriate cooperative damage assessment activities during marine spill incidents involving vessels for which they insure (about 95% of all vessels afloat). This cooperation continues in 2013 with representatives of the P&I Clubs coming to meet with Restoration Program officials in April 2013 to discuss issues such as spill preparedness, shipping in the Arctic, risks of shipping of tar sands oil/bitumen, and cooperative training opportunities.

The Restoration Program Office continues the deployment and use of improved information technology tools in 2013 by increased use of video-conferencing and developing program document libraries and document collaboration tools on the Program's SHAREPOINT site. These improvements and the enhanced use of information technology by the Program Office has resulted in reduced travel costs, consistent with Secretarial and Administration priorities while increasing internal communications efficiency.

2014 Program Performance:

All current Program Management efforts and activities are focused on providing the tools, processes, or infrastructure to achieving restoration of injured natural resources. In 2014, in compliance with Administration's Executive Order on *Campaign to Cut Waste*, the Program Office will seek to meet target goals by broadening its use of information technology in communicating with the program's workgroup, Bureaus, State, tribal, and other Federal agency partners as follows:

- Combining the use of DOI video conferencing, webinar, and SharePoint enterprise software technology. This technology will be used for all monthly meetings of the Program's Work Group to discuss program and policy issues affecting new and ongoing damage assessment projects and policies. It will also be used for the annual allocation of funding for assessment projects, eliminating face-to-face meetings in DC and/or Denver and, thereby saving travel expenses and time of Work Group members.

- The SharePoint enterprise software has been developed into a case Record Management System for the Program Office, affording Departmental bureaus and offices access to historical documents, including funding proposals dating back to 1999 as well as the attendant allocation memoranda and other supporting program documents. Further, the Program's document library within the SharePoint system currently contains over 2,000 documents that have been generated by this program such as Pre-Assessment Screen, Assessment Plans, Restoration Plans, and Consent Decrees. All of these documents are stored in the library in "searchable" .pdf file format. What was previously a vast collection of information is becoming useful data, organized and searchable.

- The organization and standardization of damage assessment project data thus allows the Program to track assessment projects' performance, and the attainment of important case milestones. Such project performance data then serves as an objective basis for future funding decisions.

- Enhanced and improved presentation and information on the Program's website (http://www.doi.gov/restoration) by improved design, accessibility, and content. A calendar of events feature has been added to inform the public of upcoming events related to public review of assessment and restoration plans, public meetings, and restoration site dedications.

The 2014 request level will support the broadened Departmental communication, consultation, and coordination activities with Federal, State, and tribal co-trustees, the environmental community, industry and the public. Continued cooperation, coordination, and collaboration with co-trustees is critical to increasing restoration productivity, and will enhance opportunities for efficiencies and to identify and eliminate duplication of effort and process redundancies.

Program management activities in 2014 will also continue efforts to develop, refine and update a number of existing administrative and policy tools, with an eye towards improved consistency, effectiveness, and maximizing restoration outcomes. Among these efforts are the following:

- Continue to evaluate the appropriate role and use of natural resource economic analytical tools and methodologies used in damage assessment and restoration activities.
- Coordinate with other trustees and restoration funding entities (U.S. Coast Guard's National Pollution Funds Center) to continue the development of common cost documentation practices and formats to ensure consistency and uniformity.
- Broaden the opportunities for cooperative assessment by improving existing guidance and documents.
- Continue improvement of public outreach and information sharing through internet-based applications and websites.
- Adopt procedures that promote coordination between response and NRDAR activities.
- Ensure that compliance by federal trustees with the requirements of the National Environmental Policy Act (NEPA) occurs concurrently with restoration planning.
- Enhance its NRDAR partnerships, through improvements in grants, cooperative agreements, and contracting.
- Encourage the use of existing local and regional restoration plans and natural resource databases for use in NRDAR restoration efforts.

Continued development and broader use of these and other tools will help ensure cross-bureau consistency and compatibility of information and systems, allowing the program to serve as a model for integrated Department-wide natural resources management.

The Program continues to enjoy a good relationship with the other Federal agencies involved in NRDAR activities either directly (i.e. NOAA, Forest Service, and NPFC) or indirectly (i.e. EPA and DOE). The Program will explore opportunities for additional collaboration and coordination, particularly in the area of project prioritization and selection. In 2014, the program will continue to reach out to industry by participating in industry symposia and discussion groups on NRDAR issues and policy, and encouraging the use of cooperative damage assessments.

As a cost-saving measure in response to diminished travel budgets, started in 2011and continuing into 2014 and beyond, the Restoration Program will transition from sponsoring its annual national workshop to a biennial schedule. Through this workshop, DOI has provided training for over 180 practitioners from across the Department on a variety of topics including project management, damage claim development, restoration methods and other scientific and legal issues. As an indicator of collaborative approach that continues to be pursued by the Department and its co-trustees, over 50 State, tribal, and Federal co-trustees, as well as representatives from industry and the conservation community also attended the most recent workshop.

Section 405 Compliance

Program Support of Bureau, Department, and Government-wide Costs:

Section 405 of the 2012 Consolidated Appropriations Act (P.L. 112-74) directs the disclosure of overhead, administrative, and other types of administrative support spending. The provision requires that budgets disclose current amounts and practices with regard to overhead charges, deductions, reserves, or holdbacks from program funding to support government-wide, Departmental, or bureau administrative functions or headquarters, regional, or central office operations. Changes to such estimates trigger reprogramming procedures, in which the Department must provide advance notice to and seek approval from the House and Senate Appropriations Committees.

For 2014, the Restoration Program's costs related to overhead, administration, and central/regional operations are addressed in three components of the budget, all under the heading of External Administrative Costs. These costs include amounts paid to bureaus, the Department, or other Executive Branch agencies to support bureau, Departmental or Government-wide administrative costs.

External Administrative Costs
(Dollars in Thousands)

	FY2012 Actual	FY2013 CR	FY 2014 Request
DOI Working Capital Fund			
Centralized Billings	99	99	122
Fee for Services	0	0	0
Direct Billings (Financial Mgmt)	152	165	165
Reimbursables	0	0	0
Total, DOI Working Capital Fund	251	264	287
DOI Interior Business Center			
Financial Managment Systems Support	5	5	5
Fish and Wildlife Service			
FWS User-Pay Cost Share	552	921	849
Bureau of Safety and Environmental Enforcement			
Personnel / HR Services	26	28	28
U.S. Geological Survey			
Common Services Support	40	50	50
U.S. Department of Justice			
DOJ Sec. 108 3% Offset Authority	51	100	100

Charges related to the Departmental Working Capital Fund (WCF) identified in the preceding table reflect the Restoration Program's share of centralized Departmental expenses for items and expenses such as telecommunications, security, mailroom services, costs associated with audited financial statements, and other WCF charges.

The Fish and Wildlife Service (FWS) levies its User-Pay Cost Share charges on damage assessment and restoration funds provided to the Service from the Restoration Program. Funds collected by FWS are used to offset a range of Servicewide administrative costs. For 2013, User-Pay Cost Share charges to the Restoration Program are estimated to be $865,872. The amounts identified for FY 2013 and 2014 are estimates based on prior year workload, and the actual amounts recovered may be more or less, depending upon actual workload, the timing of settlements, and the ability to recover such costs through settlement negotiations. Indirect costs will not be assessed to previous settlements or in cases where FWS indirect costs were not included or recovered in the final settlement. For 2014, FWS estimates those charges payable by the DOI Restoration Program to be $849,047.

Charges related to the Bureau of Safety and Environmental Enforcement (formerly Minerals Management Service) identified in the preceding table reflect the Restoration Program's share of personnel management and human resources (HR) services provided to the Office of the Secretary, covering items such as HR policies and procedures, staffing and delegated examining, employee classification, SES appointments, personnel security, reorganizations, and reductions-in-force.

The U.S. Geological Survey (USGS) applies a seven percent administrative overhead charge to all funds provided to USGS, primarily to the Columbia Environmental Research Center. Funds collected by the Center are used to offset common client administrative and facility expenses. Funds provided to USGS from the Exxon Valdez Oil Spill settlement include a nine percent general administrative assessment.

The Department of Justice applies a three percent offset to some, but not all, civil litigation debt collections made on behalf of the Restoration Program. Authority for these offsets can be found in Section 108 of the Commerce, Justice, and State Appropriations Act for Fiscal Year 1994 (P.L. 103-121, 107 Stat 1164 (1994). The offset is applicable to collections where the Department is the sole recipient of the funds. Funds subject to the offset authority are credited to the DOJ Working Capital Fund. The DOJ offset authority does not apply to restoration settlements jointly shared with non-Federal co-trustees that are collected by DOJ and deposited into the DOI Restoration Fund.

The Program Management activity, which includes Restoration Program administrative functions and central and regional operations, does not assess or levy any internal program overhead charges, deductions, or holdbacks to support such program operations.

DEPARTMENT OF THE INTERIOR
NATURAL RESOURCE DAMAGE ASSESSMENT AND RESTORATION
RESTORATION FUND

Program and Financing (in thousands of dollars)

Identification code 14-1618-0-1-302	2012 Actual	2013 Full Year CR (P.L. 112-175)	2014 Request
Obligations by program activity:			
Direct Program:			
0001 Damage Assessments	29,293	18,000	12,000
0002 Prince William Sound Restoration	1,337	2,000	2,000
0003 Other Restoration	42,730	47,000	63,000
0004 Program Management	3,874	3,000	3,000
0005 Oil Spill Preparedness	0	0	2,200
0900 Total, Direct program	77,234	70,000	82,200
Budgetary resources available for obligation:			
1000 Unobligated balance carried forward, Oct. 1	499,112	539,517	549,669
1010 Unobligated balance transferred to other accounts	-7,735	-8,051	-8,050
(Funds Transferrred to DOC/NOAA 13-4316)	[-7,515]	[-8,000]	[-8,000]
(Funds Transferrred to Forest Service 12-9921)	[-221]	[-50]	[-50]
1021 Recoveries of prior year unpaid obligations	907	0	0
1050 Unobligated balance (total)	492,284	531,466	541,619
Budget Authority			
Appropriations, discretionary			
1100 Appropriation	6,253	6,253	12,539
Appropriations, mandatory			
1201 Appropriation (Special fund)	125,493	90,000	80,000
1220 Appropriation transferred to other accounts	-7,279	-8,050	-8,050
(Funds Transferrred to DOC/NOAA 13-4316)	[-7,279]	[-8,000]	[-8,000]
(Funds Transferrred to Forest Service 12-9921)	[0]	[-50]	[-50]
1260 Appropriations (mandatory) total	118,214	81,950	71,950
1900 Budget Authority (total)	124,467	88,203	84,489
1930 Total budgetary resources available	616,751	619,669	626,108
Memorandum (non-add) entries:			
1941 Unobligated balance carried forward, end of year:	539,517	549,669	543,908
Change in obligated balance:			
Obligated balance, start of year (net):			
3000 Unpaid obligations, brought forward, Oct. 1 (gross)	20,079	25,951	19,698
3030 Obligations incurred, unexpired accounts	77,234	70,000	82,200
3040 Outlays, gross (-)	-70,455	-76,253	-85,653
3080 Recoveries of prior year unpaid obligations (-)	-907	0	0
Obligated balance, end of year (net):			
3090 Unpaid obligations, end of year (gross)	25,951	19,698	16,245
3100 Obligated balance, end of year (net)	25,951	19,698	16,245

DEPARTMENT OF THE INTERIOR
NATURAL RESOURCE DAMAGE ASSESSMENT AND RESTORATION
RESTORATION FUND

Program and Financing (in thousands of dollars) Identification code 14-1618-0-1-302	2012 Actual	2013 Full Year CR (P.L. 112-175)	2014 Request
Budget authority and outlays, net:			
Discretionary:			
4000 Budget authority, gross	6,253	6,253	12,539
Outlays, gross			
4010 Outlays from new discretionary authority	2,851	4,377	8,777
4011 Outlays from discretionary balances	2,402	1,876	1,876
4020 Outlays, gross (total)	5,253	6,253	10,653
Mandatory:			
4090 Budget authority, gross	118,214	81,950	71,950
Outlays, gross			
4100 Outlays from new mandatory authority	39,086	16,000	7,000
4101 Outlays from mandatory balances	26,116	54,000	68,000
4110 Outlays, gross (total)	65,202	70,000	75,000
Net budget authority and outlays:			
4180 Budget authority	124,467	88,203	84,489
4190 Outlays	70,455	76,253	85,653
Investments in U.S. securities			
5000 Total investments, start of year			
U.S. securities, par value	443,855	133,171	525,000
5001 Total investments, end of year			
U.S. securities, par value	133,171	525,000	525,000

Standard Form 300

DEPARTMENT OF THE INTERIOR
NATURAL RESOURCE DAMAGE ASSESSMENT AND RESTORATION
RESTORATION FUND

Program and Financing (in thousands of dollars)

Identification code 14-1618-0-1-302	2012 Actual	2013 Full Year CR (P.L. 112-175)	2014 Request
DIRECT OBLIGATIONS			
Personnel compensation:			
11.1 Full-time permanent	896	948	2,550
11.3 Other than full-time permanent	79	0	0
11.5 Other personnel compensation	9	5	10
11.9 Total personnel compensation	984	953	2,560
12.1 Civilian personnel benefits	259	275	765
21.0 Travel and transportation of persons	42	35	50
22.0 Transportation of things	0	0	2
23.1 Rental payments to GSA	126	135	200
23.3 Communications, utilities, & misc. charges	5	5	7
24.0 Printing and reproduction	1	1	2
25.2 Other services	106	150	750
25.3 Purchases of goods & services from other govt. accts	18,379	16,800	14,800
26.0 Supplies and materials	5	5	15
31.0 Equipment	2	5	10
42.0 Insurance claims and indemnities	14,423	12,886	16,300
99.9 Subtotal, direct obligations	34,332	31,250	35,461
ALLOCATION ACCOUNTS			
Personnel compensation:			
11.1 Full-time permanent	7,259	6,100	7,800
11.3 Other than full-time permanent	2,017	1,800	2,600
11.5 Other personnel compensation	443	300	300
11.8 Special personnel services payment	4	0	0
11.9 Total personnel compensation	9,723	8,200	10,700
12.1 Civilian personnel benefits	2,904	2,400	3,120
21.0 Travel and transportation of persons	1,041	800	800
22.0 Transportation of things	225	50	8
23.1 Rental payments to GSA	78	100	160
23.2 Rental payments to others	19	20	20
23.3 Communications, utilities, & misc. charges	62	60	65
24.0 Printing and reproduction	15	6	7
25.1 Advisory and assistance services	41	50	70
25.2 Other services	16,989	13,850	15,900
25.3 Purchases of goods & services from other govt. accts	1,234	1,700	2,000
25.4 Operation & maintenance of facilities	107	114	50
25.5 Research and development contracts	141	50	50
25.7 Operation & maintenance of equipment	31	50	50
26.0 Supplies and materials	665	600	600
31.0 Equipment	351	200	200
32.0 Land and structures	2,542	2,700	2,939
41.0 Grants	7,024	7,800	10,000
44.0 Refunds	-290	0	0
99.0 Subtotal obligations - Allocation Accounts	42,902	38,750	46,739
99.9 Total new obligations	77,234	70,000	82,200

DEPARTMENT OF THE INTERIOR
NATURAL RESOURCE DAMAGE ASSESSMENT AND RESTORATION
RESTORATION FUND

Program and Financing (in thousands of dollars)

Identification code 14-1618-0-1-302	2012 Actual	2013 Full Year CR (P.L. 112-175)	2014 Request
Obligations are distributed as follows:			
Natural Resource Damage Assessment Program Office	34,332	31,250	35,461
Bureau of Indian Affairs	986	1,000	1,000
Bureau of Land Management	694	700	700
Bureau of Reclamation	64	100	200
Fish and Wildlife Service	29,203	27,550	35,439
National Park Service	6,273	5,000	5,000
Office of the Secretary	334	400	400
U.S. Geological Survey	5,348	4,000	4,000
99.9 Total new obligations	77,234	70,000	82,200

Personnel Summary

Identification code 14-1618-0-1-302	2012 Actual	2013 Full Year CR (P.L. 112-175)	2014 Request
Direct:			
Total compensable workyears:			
1001 Full-time equivalent employment	9	12	20

DEPARTMENT OF THE INTERIOR
NATURAL RESOURCE DAMAGE ASSESSMENT AND RESTORATION
EMPLOYEE COUNT BY GRADE

	2012 Actual	2013 CR	2014 Estimate
Executive Level	0	0	0
SES..	1	1	1
CA-3 *...	0	0	0
AL-2-3 **...	0	0	0
SL-0 ***...	0	0	0
subtotal..............	1	1	1
GS/GM-15	1	1	1
GS/GM-14	2	2	2
GS/GM-13	4	5	7
GS-12	0	1	4
GS-11	0	1	3
GS-10	0	0	0
GS-9	0	1	1
GS-8	0	0	0
GS-7	1	0	1
GS-6	0	0	0
GS-5	0	0	0
GS-4	0	0	0
GS-3	0	0	0
GS-2	0	0	0
subtotal (GS/GM)..............	8	11	19
Total employment (actual / projected) at end of fiscal year......................	9	12	20

*CA - DOI Board Member
**AL - Administrative Law Judge
***SL - Senior-Level / Scientific Professionals